Forty Years
with
the
.45-70

by Paul A. Matthews

Manufactured in the United States of America

All rights reserved. No part of this book may be used or reproduced in any manner whatsoever without prior written permission from the publisher except by a reviewer who wishes to quote brief passages in connection with a review.

Queries regarding rights and permissions should be addressed to:
Wolfe Publishing Company
6471 Airpark Drive
Prescott, Arizona 86301

Wolfe Publishing Company is not responsible for mishaps of any nature which might occur from use of published data in this book.

Wolfe Publishing Company
ISBN: 0-935632-84-0
Copyright ©1989

The author with a wild boar he shot with a Ruger No. 3 .45-70 and a 450-grain paper patched bullet backed by 53 grains of IMR-3031. The boar dropped in its tracks. *(Photo by Frank M. Matthews)*

Warning!

This book contains loads that I developed or used in various .45-70 rifles over the past forty years. And although these loads were apparently safe for the rifles I used them in, they may be dangerous in your rifle. I have included these loads merely for the information therein, and neither I nor the publisher of this book will assume any responsibility for injury or damage resulting from the use of any load or loading procedure described in this book. If you choose to use the loads and follow the loading procedures described in this book, you are strictly on your own.

Paul A. Matthews
January 30, 1989

Dedication

To my dear wife Betty who for more than forty years has stood by me, and on a day in May of 1950 in Andy Spina's Trading Post at Towanda, Pennsylvania, encouraged me to fork over the majority of my paycheck — the third I had earned after being out of work for fifteen and one-half months — for a Winchester Model 1886 .45-70 rifle having a new barrel installed and chambered by Parker O. Ackley. Such women as she are far scarcer and more treasured than fine rifles. To Betty, I most sincerely dedicate this book.

Table of Contents

Acknowledgments 9
Introduction 11
  1 The Seed Is Planted......................13
  2 The Search 17
  3 The Gould Bullet........................23
  4 The Postell Bullet and a Springfield 33
  5 Back to the Gould Bullet 37
  6 Jacketed Bullets and a Few Deer 43
  7 A Question of Pressure 49
  8 Multiple Bullet Load 53
  9 Looking for a Single Shot..................57
10 The Two Rugers 63
11 More Deer with the No. 1 69
12 Back to the Ruger No. 3 75
13 Search for a Cast Bullet 77
14 RCBS, Old West and Hoch Moulds 83
15 Paper Patched Bullets 89
16 Deer and Wild Boar.......................97
17 Patching Grooved Bullets 107
18 Other Moulds and Loads 111
19 Powders 117
20 The Final Word 123
21 Letters 127

Acknowledgments

No man goes through life alone, nor does he ever accomplish anything solely by his own efforts. In this life he is influenced by others, helped or hindered, encouraged or discouraged, but in sum total influenced all the way.

Probably the one man who has helped me the most over the years is Charles H. Canoll. Forty years ago as an accomplished gunsmith and toolmaker, Charlie gave me much good advice along with the loan of many bullet moulds and an occasional gunsmith job on whatever rifle was my choice at the time. Of late years, Charlie has made a number of special bullet moulds for me, paper patch moulds and otherwise. To Charlie Canoll I owe a lot.

Then of course there are many others, mostly writers, to whom I wrote for information — men like Elmer Keith, M. D. "Bud" Waite, A. H. Barr, Phil Sharpe, Tom Florich, Parker O. Ackley, Jack O'Connor and finally, one whom I knew on a personal basis, Henry M. Stebbins. These men gave generously of their time and hard-earned information.

And in later years whenever I needed a special front sight made or an adapter to accommodate a rear receiver sight for a rifle for which no such sight was available, I have immense gratitude for two other fine machinists: Harold C. Reynolds and Fred Cornell. To these men I am truly indebted.

I am also certain that somewhere, someplace over these past forty years there are other faces, other voices and other names lost in the swirl of time, but nonetheless faces, voices and names that in one way or another influenced my life with the .45-70. To these, too, I am humbly grateful.

Paul A. Matthews
January 30, 1989

Introduction

This is not a history of the .45-70 cartridge. That has already been written numerous times by more knowledgeable persons than myself. Nor is it a history of the old Trapdoor Springfield or any other rifle chambered for that venerable cartridge. For that information you can read Jack Behn's fine book *.45-70 Rifles* or *The Trapdoor Springfield* by B. D. Ernst and M. D. "Bud" Waite. And if you want to read something strictly on handloading this cartridge for the various rifles, then you can do no better than to read Ken Waters' fine two-part article in the seventh edition of the *Handloader's Digest* and in *Handloader* magazine Nos. 48 and 49.

This little book's intention is to relate my personal experiences with a number of different .45-70 rifles over the past four decades. Some of the things I did during those years were rather harebrained and certainly should never be repeated. Other things were done in the interest of gaining knowledge, and still others were to utilize the full potential of the cartridge — a goal that few, if any, have ever achieved. In short then, this little book is pure gun lore — lore of the .45-70.

1

The Seed Is Planted

When I looked back up the hill, the buck was there, his head turned staring down at me and his body partially obscured by brush. I caught a glimpse of antler and, without even standing, pivoted around on the stump. The little Ruger No. 3 .45-70 found my shoulder and the instant the crosshairs settled at the juncture of the neck and body, I pressed the trigger. The whole thing didn't take more than three seconds, but it had been nearly half a lifetime in the making.

I cannot put a specific date on the starting point because my first letter from Elmer Keith sometime back in 1949 is lost forever. But I do recall his kind remarks and the trigger mechanism that had sparked them.

I was a .30-06 man then, the proud owner of a spanking new Winchester Model 70 (serial 89,722) equipped with a Lyman 48WJS receiver sight. I thought a lot of that rifle and Elmer Keith had given the cartridge what I considered to be a severe panning. In my youthful brashness I wrote Elmer a letter that would curl hair, and when the reply came I expected the envelope to be smoking of hellfire and brimstone.

Quite the opposite was the case, because Elmer knew what he was talking about and didn't feel that he had to enter a shouting contest to make himself heard. Softly and gently he told me that more people agreed with me than with him, and that in my own wisdom probably the right thing to do

— if I ever had the chance — was to shoot a big bore rifle myself and then make up my own mind. To hell with the experts!

The opportunity came a few days later when Charlie Canoll, on an invitation to a Sunday dinner, showed up at the house with a couple of Mills belts full of old smokeless government loads, an almost perfect Remington-Keene bolt action hammer gun and an equally good condition Trapdoor Springfield carbine.

Now the ammunition that Charlie had was, as I recall, originally made for Gatling gun use. It carried a 500-grain lead bullet and a charge of smokeless powder. In those days such government surplus ammunition was available at a remarkably low price from a number of sources such as Public Sports Shops of Philadelphia, Hudson Sporting Goods Company of New York and many others. In fact, a December 1948 issue of the *American Rifleman* lists .405 Winchester ammunition at $17.54 per 100 rounds from Hudson Sporting Goods and .45-70 black powder cartridges at $10.00 per 100 from Public Sports Shops. Those days are forever gone!

At any rate my shooting range at that time was in my dad's cow pasture where a long-dead native chestnut tree three to four feet in diameter served as a backstop. We had a spike driven into the tree and from this hung a plow wheel about a foot in diameter and made of a very tough, abrasion-resistant steel about $5/16$-inch thick. Bullets from my '06 punched a nice clean hole through the wheel with hardly a quiver.

Sometime during the course of our shooting that day, Charlie handed me one of the .45-70s and a beltful of ammunition. That, friends, was my moment of truth. Whichever rifle I used, it shot true, the heavy slug striking the wheel with a loud "clang" and then *throwing* the wheel from the tree for a distance of about twenty feet! Examination of the wheel showed that the 500-grain bullet had made a bulge about the size of a hen's egg, and in the bottom of the bulge was a large crack where the lead had squirted on through. Elmer Keith had made his point. By comparison, my '06 seemed puny.

We fired every round of .45-70 ammo that Charlie had. His

Remington-Keene was exceptionally accurate and shot the old government ammo just as close as I could hold.

A dirt road ran along the cow pasture, and in the fenceline there was an old pine tree probably eighteen inches in diameter. I looked at it for a moment and then asked Charlie if the .45-70 would shoot through the tree. His reply was to try it. I did and it did, and I could hardly believe what I was seeing. I knew there was no way the '06 was going to shove an expanding bullet through that tree. Long before Charlie left that day, I knew that someday, somehow, I had to have a good .45-70 rifle.

Charles H. Canoll at his lathe in his gunsmithing establishment at Waverly, New York, in 1955. Charlie gave the author a firsthand introduction to the .45-70 cartridge and rifle in 1949, an act that greatly influenced the author's choice of calibers from that day on.

2

The Search

Now in those days just after World War II, I was out of work. I had been laid off on December 31, 1948, and didn't get back to work until April 17, 1950. How I managed to pay for the Winchester '06 in February 1949, I don't recall, but pay for it I did, and in the summer of 1949 I hunted woodchucks with an obsession and my wife canned them for the coming winter. That fall I also shot my first deer with the '06 using a Speer 180-grain bullet backed with 43 grains of 3031.

In a letter from A. H. Barr of the *American Rifleman* staff, Mr. Barr questioned my choice of powder for such a heavy bullet. I could have told him. I got more loads per pound than with a slower burning powder, and at that time in my life the few extra loads made a difference.

As soon as I got called back to work, I started looking for a Winchester 1886 .45-70. Every town had its secondhand shop and the one in Towanda was called the Trading Post. I loved to haunt those places because they were a tangible link with the past, but that day when I walked into the Trading Post, the first thing I asked Andy Spina was, "Have you got any .45-70 rifles?"

In the back of the room, from a cabinet secluded in an obscure corner, Andy handed me a Winchester 1886 with a brand new barrel by P. O. Ackley, and a blue job second to none.

"How much?"

"Seventy dollars."

I hadn't drawn my first paycheck yet, and seventy dollars seemed an astronomical sum. In my pocket I had a ten spot.

"How long will you hold the rifle for ten dollars?"

Andy looked at me and smiled. "I'd hold it forever," he said.

And in my ear, Betty whispered, "You better do it!"

Most of my third paycheck went to pay the balance for that rifle and a couple boxes of handloads that Andy threw in.

At that time we lived in an old farmhouse sans running water and bathroom facilities. It was perched high on the side of a hill with a front porch nearly ten feet off the ground and six or eight wooden steps leading down. I sat on one of those steps with that Winchester to take my first shot at a target seventy yards distant. To this day I can remember the surge of exhilaration as I levered the action and dropped one of those watermelon cartridges in that gaping chamber. Then I squinted along the barrel aligning the ivory bead front sight with the "V" notch in the rear, and then the two of them together with the target.

When I pressed the trigger, it was like getting hit in the pit of the stomach. That old curved rifle buttplate, beautiful as it was on that highly finished stock, was pure murder from anything except the offhand position. Offhand, the rifle held rock-steady and was easy to shoot. In fact, I once cranked five rounds through that gun in twelve seconds and kept them all in a six-inch bull at fifty yards. That was when firepower was important to me.

One of the highly touted cast bullet loads in those days was 20 grains of 4759 powder behind the Ideal 457124 bullet, the standard 405-grain military bullet. Ballistic data from the H. P. White Laboratory printed in the November 1950 issue of the *American Rifleman* shows 867 fps velocity for this load — an extremely mild dose for such a large cartridge. As I recall, that was the load used in the cartridges Andy Spina had given me.

In those days if you wanted new empty cases, you bought factory ammunition. The ammunition manufacturers frowned on reloading and their components were not readily available. Thus it was that for the next four or five weeks, every paycheck had a bite out of it for a box of cartridges. But instead of shooting the stuff, I pulled the bullets and saved them for hunting.

Charlie Canoll showed me how to pull .45-70 bullets without damaging them — and this was long before the inertia bullet pullers. Taking a piece of oak about an inch thick, an inch-and-a-half wide and eighteen inches long, Charlie drilled a half-inch hole through it close to one end. I'd stick a loaded .45-70 cartridge through the hole, loop a rubber band over the rim to hold the cartridge in place, and then rap the piece of oak over a chunk of firewood set on end. One or two raps and I'd catch the bullet and powder in my hand.

With the price of factory ammunition (or even surplus ammunition) being more than I could afford to satisfy my shooting appetite, Betty again came to the rescue and agreed that I should order an Ideal 310 loading tool for the .45-70. I already had one for the '06.

For those who have never owned or used an Ideal 310 reloading tool, it is difficult to imagine just how uncomplicated and handy the little nutcracker tool was. No, it wasn't on a par with the big Hollywood press I bought a short time later, but the Ideal 310 was an excellent tool for the money and turned out some first-rate ammunition. I still have the dies for my old 310 and use them with thread adapters in my Hollywood press.

I was working nights at the time, usually getting home about 2:30 in the morning, and to pass away the time during the long evenings, Betty often reloaded my ammunition for me. Television was so far in the future for us that it wasn't even a dream.

Where the .45-70 was concerned, just getting the 310 tool did not solve all my problems. I had to have bullets, lots of them, so I went to Charlie and borrowed a couple of moulds. One was for a Marlin 500-grain and the other was an old metal handle, rigid block mould for the standard 405-grain military bullet. The Marlin mould was in fine condition, whereas the other showed a slight fin at the nose and some irregularities around the base.

Lead was plentiful. Where I worked, we used lead hammers to nudge parts into place in lathe chucks, and every place you looked you could find misshapened and battered hammer heads lying around. I had no problem getting twenty pounds of beat up hammer heads in my aluminum lunch bucket, and after I explained to the foreman what I was doing, he often laid a battered hammer head on my workbench. For a budding reloader with a frail pocketbook, it was a bonanza!

With plenty of bullet metal available, moulds I'd borrowed from Charlie Canoll, and a cast iron kettle salvaged from a junk pile, I was in business. I converted a chicken coop to my "gunsmith shop" and built a coal-fired casting furnace from a fifty-pound pail, two ten-quart pails and some asbestos. With that outfit I could melt forty pounds of alloy with no problem. Later I purchased a gasoline plumber's furnace from Sears Roebuck and used it for the next thirty years. This, too, would handle forty pounds of alloy and get it far hotter than the coal furnace I had built.

I cast bullets by the hundreds (thousands?) and shot them almost as fast as I cast them. Most of my loads were either of 4759, or Elmer Keith's old standard of 53 grains of 3031.

The Winchester Model 1886 purchased from Andy Spina in April 1950. At the time of purchase this rifle had been rebarreled by Parker O. Ackley and chambered for the .45-70. Inletting of the forearm indicates that the rifle originally had an octagon barrel, while the serial number indicates manufacture sometime in 1893 or 1894. This fine rifle is now owned by the author's son, George.

In the early 1950s the author purchased this gasoline plumber's furnace for his bullet casting operations. This furnace will easily melt forty pounds of bullet alloy and keep it hot enough for casting. Today the author uses a number of different heat sources for bullet casting, including a Lyman Mould Master modified for dipping, a Coleman Model 508 camp stove and a propane plumber's furnace with a twenty-pound tank.

3

The Gould Bullet

Neither of the bullets from the moulds I had borrowed from Charlie suited me. First, they were from borrowed moulds, and I didn't like to borrow moulds. Second, the Marlin bullet seemed excessively heavy while the 405-grain bullet from the other mould was considerably less than perfect. By now I had accumulated enough brass to last me for awhile, so I convinced Betty that I just had to have a new bullet mould — one of my own.

In those days I could post an order to Lyman on one Friday and receive my goods the next Friday, this through the good old U.S. mail. I have forgotten exactly what a set of mould blocks cost at that time, but I think it was around $5.00. At any rate, I had read quite a bit about the 330-grain Gould hollowpoint bullet. It was on Lyman's list of special bullets (extra price) in *Handbook No. 35*, and I ordered one.

At that time the Gould bullet was listed as No. 456122 and my mould blocks are so stamped. Today it is listed as No. 457122. Whether this is because there was a wide variation in barrel dimensions, or whether .45-70 barrels were supposed to be smaller than today's .458-inch diameter, I don't know. I do know that the Gould bullet is excellent for use on deer. That is what Mr. A. C. Gould wanted and that is how John H. Barlow designed it. Somewhere I've read that Barlow actually designed two other similar bullets, one lighter and one heavier, but the 330-grain was the one that Gould selected.

I have also read that at one time the cavity in the bullet nose was large enough to accept a .22 blank cartridge to make an explosive bullet. I've never seen such a mould and the hollowpoint pin in my mould is much smaller in diameter and has a slight taper. However, I believe that this may have been the case with some of the early moulds, perhaps on special order, as my mould casts a bullet somewhat heavier than 330 grains when using a soft alloy.

The Gould hollowpoint opened up entire new vistas for me. It was a honey in that Winchester, accurate and deadly. In a lead-tin mixture of 16 to 1 it cast easily and was soft enough for positive expansion. Backed by 53 grains of 3031 or 54 grains of the surplus 4895 powders available through the DCM (Director of Civilian Marksmanship) at the time, it gave superb accuracy with only a trace of leading in the barrel.

In order to eliminate the leading, I purchased a .45-caliber Osborne Wadcutter available from Belding & Mull at the time for $1.10. With this I cut thin felt wads from an old hat and dipped them in melted lube, later seating them between the powder and the base of the bullet. This virtually eliminated all of the leading except on bitter cold days while deer hunting. Later Emmer Keith advised me that I'd probably be better off using eighth-inch cork gasket material as it would better protect the base of the bullet from gas cutting and from deformation by kernels of powder slamming against it.

Keith's objection to the greased felt was that it might contaminate the powder, depending upon what grease or mixture was used. He said that he himself liked to use felt wads in cap and ball revolvers, but that he dipped his wads in either beeswax or tallow — something that wouldn't migrate.

There is a lot to his thinking. Later on in the game, I used tallow wads, some from beef tallow and some from deer tallow. Those from deer tallow were much harder than the beef and were far less likely to migrate into the powder.

As for bullet lubricant, this was long before the day of our standard Alox/beeswax mixture. I used the Lyman lube with graphite to some extent, but then switched to my own mixture of almost anything that would melt mixed with liberal amounts of finely powdered graphite. If the resultant mixture was too hard, I added water-pump grease. If it was too soft, I added beeswax. If it was too light colored, I added graphite. As haphazard as it sounds, it seemed to work.

I had no sizer-lubricator in those days, so lubed all of my bullets by the old pie-pan melted-lubricant method, and peeled off the excess with a Kake Kutter made by drilling through the head of a fired .45-70 case. Then I machined a sizing die through which I forced all of my bullets, helped along by a flat-faced punch. Bullets often went through the die nose-first. If they had a flat nose, like the Gould bullet, then I sized them base-first.

Naturally this sizing and lubricating process was time-consuming and maybe the sizing method was not the best treatment for a soft bullet that was supposed to fly in a straight line. Thus, in an effort to save time, I came up with another idea that I first tried with the 500-grain Marlin bullet. This was simple and effective, but it too had its drawbacks.

Simply put, after charging my cases with powder and a stiff card wad (the card took up less room than the $\frac{1}{8}$-inch cork), I would put a healthy gob of water-pump grease in the case and then seat an as-cast, unlubricated bullet. As the bullet seated against the wad, the water-pump grease was forced up around the bullet and into the grease grooves. Any excess grease came out the mouth of the case into the loading die — the first drawback.

The second drawback occurred when the cartridge was fired; powder gases forced some of the grease back around the outside of the cartridge case, thus creating excessive thrust against the breechblock. Despite this, bullets so lubricated shot well with no leading, and perhaps if I could have found a firmer grease, the idea would have worked out. As it was, the water-pump grease I used then was plenty firm, far firmer than any grease I've seen available today. At any rate, for sizing and lubricating it was back to the old pie plate with melted lubricant, Kake Kutter and hand-held sizing die.

Aside from being an excellent deer bullet, the Gould

hollowpoint offers all kinds of possibilities for the fertile mind to play on. In John H. Barlow's *Ideal Handbook No. 11*, he speaks of filling the hollowpoint cavity with wax or tallow. I can only guess that this may hasten the expansion process as the filler would certainly act hydraulically at the instant of impact. Though I never tried this, I did try some other equally novel ideas.

First, after casting any number of hollowpoint bullets, I decided I would like some solid bullets from the same mould, that is, bullets without the hollow point. After trying rather unsuccessfully to make a plug for the hole in the bottom of the mould, I took to dropping a steel BB inside the mould to plug the hole normally occupied by the hollowpoint pin. It takes a little practice to do this as you cannot tip the mould while pouring the metal. But the idea worked and I produced some solid bullets with a steel BB firmly embedded in the nose.

Since the steel BB protrudes slightly from the nose of the bullet, there was no way I could use these in a tubular magazine without wrecking the rifle and myself on the first shot. With the heavy recoil involved and the cartridges laying in the magazine BB-to-primer, there is no doubt in my mind that the cartridges in the magazine would fire along with the one in the chamber.

Using another approach, I found that I could take a soft Gould hollowpoint bullet and make a Hoxie bullet out of it by pressing the steel BB into the hollowpoint until it was flush with the bullet's meplat. Whether or not there is any advantage to such a bullet is doubtful, but they were unique.

Solid-nose cast bullets can be made to expand as rapidly as the express-type hollowpoints by placing a narrow strip of thin paper between the mould blocks in the area of the bullet's nose. Then, when you cast a bullet, the nose has a split in it that greatly facilitates expansion, especially at black powder velocities or at extended ranges. One thing you don't want to do is to run the split all the way out to the end of the bullet nose as this will cause the bullet to blossom out like a hollyhock as soon as it leaves the muzzle of the rifle.

This procedure was illustrated in Barlow's early issues of the *Ideal Handbook*, as well as in the Lyman "Centennial Journal."

The first deer I ever shot with the .45-70 was taken with the Gould bullet cast 1 to 16 tin and lead, and loaded over 54 grains of surplus 4895 with a greased felt wad between the powder and the bullet base. It was nearly dark and I was headed toward home when I stepped down off a bank into the bottom of a creek bed. Glancing up the creek, there was a big doe standing broadside looking at me. In one easy motion I cocked the rifle as it came to my shoulder, and the instant the ivory bead front sight settled on her chest, I pressed the trigger.

A heavy .45-70 bullet makes a distinctive "Ker-Wunk" when it hits the chest of a deer, and even though the doe jumped out of the creek bed, I knew I had made a solid hit. I was concerned about finding her as it was nearly dark and there was no snow. However, when I got to where she had been standing, there was a blood trail a blind man could have followed. The deer lay about sixty yards away. That soft Gould bullet had gone completely through her, smashing the lower part of her heart as it went. Range was 137 paces.

One of the most famous misses of my career was also with the Winchester 1886 and the Gould bullet loaded as before. Again, it was doe season, only this time it was bitter cold and my throat felt like a piece of raw beefsteak slightly seared on one side. I knew that deer had been lying on some of the more open slopes along Mallory Run, so I poked along the rim of the slopes keeping out of sight and looking over the rim about every hundred feet or so.

Sure enough, pretty soon I looked over and there was a big doe about fifty yards away down a steep slope. She had her back to me as she watched the creek bed, and when I raised the rifle I would have bet everything I owned on that one shot. All I got was a handful of hair where the Gould bullet brushed her off-side.

With the rifle sighted in for one hundred yards, it was about three inches high at sixty yards. More than that, from my position above the doe, I was looking at her off-side and not her near-side. Had I held for the line where her body and the snow met, I'd have made my meat for the day. Years later my son Frank missed a fine buck with the same rifle under similar circumstances.

Although the Gould bullet is one of the best available for deer hunting, any prospective buyer of a mould for the bullet should first check the chamber of his rifle. A number of .45-70 rifles have considerable freebore just ahead of the chamber, requiring that the bullet jump quite a distance before it engages the rifling. This doesn't do accuracy any good, and seating the Gould bullet out further so that it just kisses the rifling exposes the forward grease groove to dirt. Rifles not having the freebore will normally handle the Gould bullet with exceptional accuracy.

Above, .45-70 cartridges and bullets used in the Winchester 1886. From left to right: *1)* a .45-caliber roundball, *2)* the 330-grain Gould hollow-point bullet, *3)* a Barnes 400-grain jacketed bullet, *4)* a shortened Postell 475-grain bullet (Lyman 457132), *5)* a factory load with a 405-grain bullet, and *6)* a Frankfort Arsenal cartridge having a tinned case and a 500-grain military bullet backed with a grease wad and black powder.

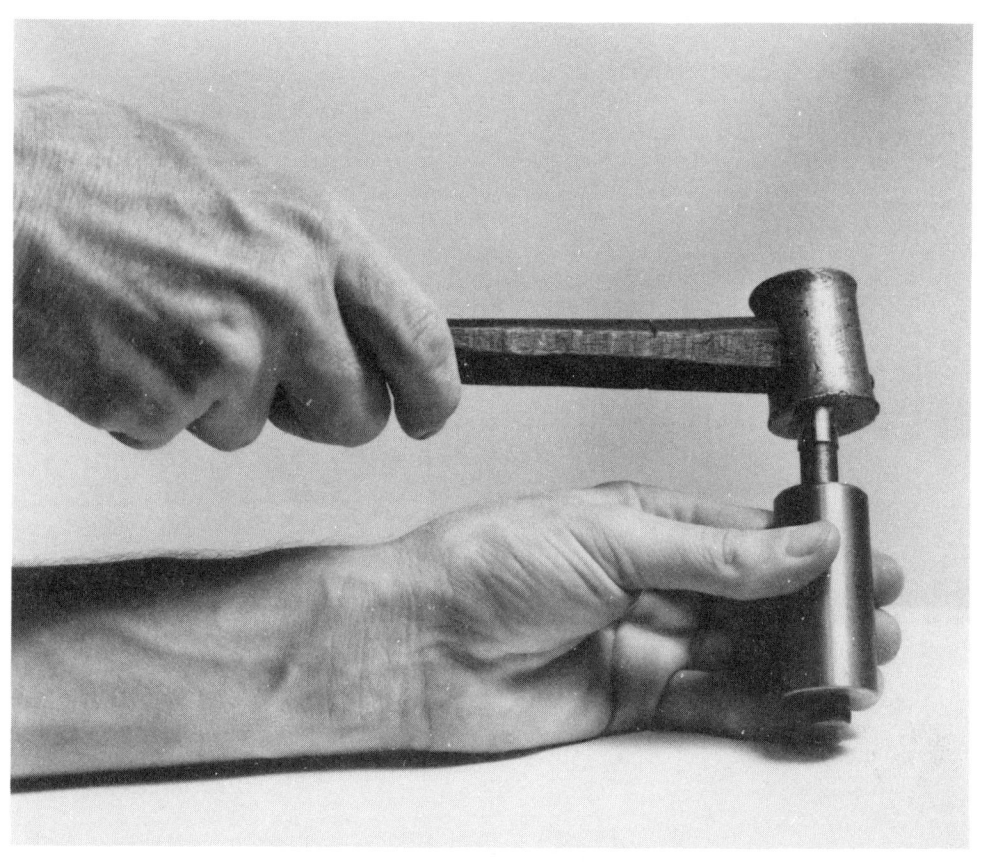

Sizing a Gould hollowpoint bullet in a hand-held sizing die made by the author. Bullets were first lubricated by standing them in a pie pan of melted lubricant, then removing them with a Kake Kutter fashioned from a fired .45-70 case.

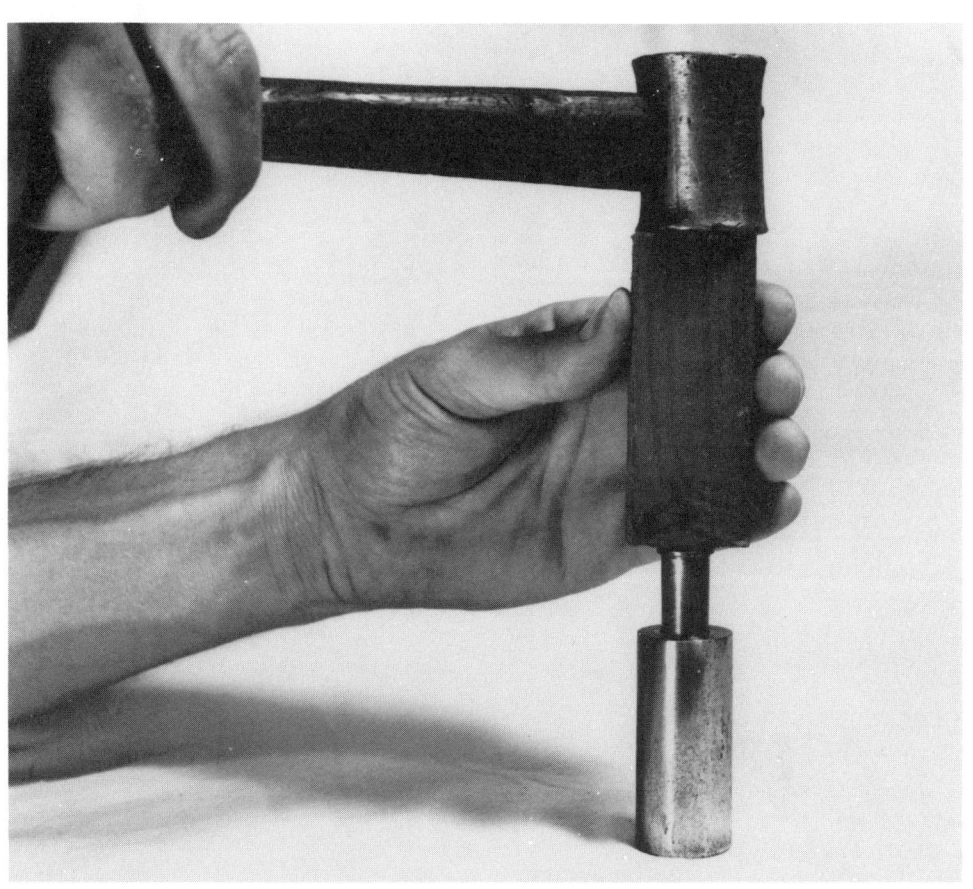

The old method used to full-length cartridge cases, and the old Lyman die did a good job. If the case was thin and the rifle chamber on the small side, the case could be driven into the die with a block of wood and hammer as shown. With heavier brass or a large chamber, it was always easier to use a bench vise.

4

The Postell Bullet and a Springfield

After I had played with the Gould bullet for awhile, I wanted a heavy one to work with — something like the Marlin 500-grain. At the time I probably would have been better off if I had purchased the Lyman 457125, a copy of the old military 500-grainer. However, wanting something a bit different, I chose the Lyman 457132 shortened by one base band. This was the old Postell bullet, or grooved version of the Sharps 550-grain paper-patched bullet. Its normal weight was 535 grains, but shortening it by one band reduced its weight to 475 grains.

The Postell bullet is a beautiful long-range bullet for a single-shot rifle where overall cartridge length does not interfere with magazines and feeding mechanisms. In a magazine rifle the long nose of the bullet makes the overall cartridge length excessive unless the bullet is seated deeply into the case. I didn't realize this until I had the mould in hand and had loaded some cartridges.

Still, the Postell bullet with its fine shape awakened a desire for a good single-shot rifle. At the time Charlie Canoll had a .45-caliber Sharps-Borchardt chambered, as I recall, for the $2\frac{7}{8}$-inch case. I borrowed this rifle and despite the fact the bullets had to jump from that short .45-70 case to engage the rifling, it shot fairly well. I remember loading up a handful of cartridges with the Postell bullet and 54 grains of 4895 and getting some pretty respectable groups. Recoil was something else, especially for a thin guy who weighed about a hundred and a quarter at the time.

After working with the Borchardt for a week or so, I started looking for a single-shot of my own and came up with an almost perfect Springfield Trapdoor carbine. I believe I paid $10.00 for that little rifle and it was going to be my black powder gun.

Actually I had already been working with black powder in the Winchester and found that the DuPont powder in use at the time made an awful mess in the barrel — long black streaks that looked about like tar. However, I also found that by using a priming charge of smokeless, most of the solids in the black powder were burned off to leave a much cleaner barrel and deliver better accuracy. Articles in the *American Rifleman* talked about using five grains of DuPont No. 5 pistol powder as a priming charge, but I felt that the same amount of 4759 did a much better job at somewhat lower pressures.

I also reasoned that if five grains of smokeless would make the main charge of FFg black powder burn cleaner, a similar charge of black could be used behind a load of 3031 to make that burn cleaner. And it did! Though I don't know what pressures were involved in the process.

At any rate, I used my duplex black powder loads in the little Springfield and had a lot of fun doing it. Charlie filed the barleycorn front sight off, soldered on a $\frac{1}{8}$-inch blade sight, and replaced the original rear sight with a fully adjustable sight taken from a Krag rifle. It made a nice outfit, but the trapdoor action did not appeal to me like the Sharps-Borchardt.

Later a friend gave me a can of Laflin and Rand Orange Extra powder that burned cleaner than the DuPont. At the same time I picked up some old UMC cases of dubious ancestry and proceeded to load them with the Orange Extra and the Postell bullet. The very first round I fired in the Springfield blew the head off the case with no damage to the rifle. That was my first and only experience with a case which I believe had once been fired with a mercuric primer.

Despite its messiness, I liked working with black powder, or at least I liked the idea of being able to load a compressed load without worrying about undue pressures. This was nearly my undoing.

Returning from a bear hunt one day, I stopped in at the Lewis Gun Shop at Towanda, Pennsylvania, to see "what was new." And there on the shelf was a can of DuPont Bulk Smokeless Shotgun powder. Now my knowledge of powders was fairly limited, and of the DuPont Bulk Smokeless Shotgun powder, I knew nothing — except that it could be used bulk for bulk with black. I had a good friend with me who should have known better but didn't, and although he agreed with the bulk for bulk loading in a shotgun, he wasn't certain how it would do in a rifle.

That evening I loaded a case with 70 grains bulk and was about to seat a Gould bullet when I decided that in the interest of safety I would cut the charge to 60 grains bulk. This done, I seated the bullet and took the Winchester and cartridge to the outhouse. While standing inside and holding the rifle one-handed outside the door, I fired it.

Both the recoil and report were pleasantly mild, and I was quite pleased with myself until I tried to open the action. It wouldn't budge. Back in the house with a ramrod down the muzzle, a few gentle taps loosened the cartridge case and opened the action. Still, on the head of the cartridge case, barely visible, was the imprint of the face of the breechblock and extractor. If you have any DuPont Bulk Smokeless Shotgun powder kicking around, it's strictly for shotguns, not rifles.

5

Back to the Gould Bullet

Still interested in a lighter load for the Gould bullet, I turned to 4227 powder. At that time I used 30 grains, probably because 32.9 grains of Sharpshooter was said to be the factory high velocity load with a 300-grain bullet. I had no idea what velocity I was getting, but because it shot a bit flatter than a factory load and was accurate, I was happy. Now that I've had some experience with the chronograph, I'd guess that load was doing about 1,500 fps. No faster.

By itself, the 30-grain load of 4227 did not burn clean. It did not begin to fill the case, so I resorted to Cream of Wheat as a filler and immediately began getting good ignition and clean burning. Since using Cream of Wheat was somewhat of a nuisance, I found it more expedient to seat one of my cork wads against the powder, thus positioning the powder against the primer and leaving an air space between the wad and the bullet's base.

In those days I don't recall ever reading of the dangers of such a practice, and I got by with it although I didn't really do a lot of shooting with cartridges so loaded. However, as we know today, leaving an air space between a wad of any kind and the base of the bullet is an excellent way to ring or bulge the rifle's chamber. You just don't do such damn fool things!

Since deer season only came once a year and you were

allowed only one deer per season, it was a bit difficult to test bullets to determine their capability. Someplace I had read about using gelatin as a test medium, and putting on my thinking cap, I remembered that in the buffing department in the plant where I worked there were barrels of the stuff in crystal form. Again, I went to the foreman and came home with at least four pounds of gelatin crystals.

After cutting the top out of a two-gallon oil can and inserting a plastic bag (they were just coming on the market then) of the proper size, I had my gelatin mould. I dissolved the crystals in water using a pretty rich mixture of crystals and poured it in the oil can to harden. This gave me a good size block of gelatin to work with, and after using it once, all I had to do to cast a new block was to heat it up to the melting point.

Even though a block of gelatin isn't a deer and doesn't react like one, I still learned a lot about bullet behavior and bullet wounds. Firing a bullet through the gelatin block would cause a violent temporary expansion of the gelatin, which in turn shredded the plastic bag longitudinally in a clearly visible pattern that looked like the shape of the wound channel inside the gelatin. To me, this was exciting and added to my knowledge. I fired many rounds through blocks of gelatin at various ranges. Two notes found on photographs from those long-ago days are significant:

"Photo 8: Wound channel of .45/70/405 handloaded utilizing Western softnose bullet and 54 grains of 4895 (lot 27277). Range 75 yards. Although the bullet did not show any signs of shedding weight, it made a wound channel comparable to the .375 H&H. Upon impact, the gelatin block jumped a good two feet into the air, spun around and landed on the ground. The gelatin was cratered and creviced radially around the major channel."

"Photo 9: Bullet wound made by .45/70 at 20 yards. Load was 30 grains of 4227 with case filled on up with Post's Wheat Meal. Bullet was 330-grain Gould hollowpoint cast 8-1-1 lead, tin and antimony. Forward portion of bullet shattered and pieces were found throughout the gelatin with many of them laying

in the wound itself. At sixty yards the load and bullet acted the same as at twenty. Should make a good deer load as the hard bullet will not lead in the wintertime and all energy will be expended within the deer. Was unable to retrieve solid base section of bullet as it angled slightly upward, missing the sawdust container. Gelatin did not jump as in photo 8."

Although today I wouldn't think of using a hard cast bullet on deer, there is a school of thought that does favor such bullet fragmentation. For those, a hard cast Gould hollow-point bullet should be the berries.

Photo 8

Wound channel in a block of gelatin. The bullet was a Western 405-grain softnose backed by 54 grains of surplus 4895 (lot 27277). Range was 75 yards.

Photo 9

Wound channel made by a Gould hollowpoint bullet backed by 30 grains of 4227. The bullet was cast of a hard 8-1-1 alloy and completely shattered within the gelatin. Range was 20 yards.

6

Jacketed Bullets and a Few Deer

Even though the Gould bullet gave very little leading, and virtually none at all during warm weather, any leading whatsoever in a rifle barrel is suspect to impaired accuracy. And although I am not primarily a target shooter, when I press the trigger in the game field I want to know that the bullet is going where the sights lay at the time the rifle is fired.

Somewhere along the line I changed the sighting system on the Winchester from the semi-buckhorn rear and ivory bead front to a Lyman 56 receiver sight and a Redfield Sourdough on front. This made for an extremely fast, accurate, steady-holding brush rifle. To go along with this change, I switched from the fragile Gould hollowpoint to the Western 405-grain jacketed bullet pulled from factory ammunition. I also purchased a quantity of roundnose 400-grain bullets from Barnes. With these latter bullets I had to file the exposed lead back to the jacket in order to get a flat nose suitable for use in a tubular magazine. With either jacketed bullet, my load was 53 grains of 3031 powder or 54 grains of 4895 (lot 27277).

Perhaps it might be worthwhile to interject a note here about the lot numbers of 4895. Surplus 4895 powder left over from World War II was available from the DCM for about $.22 a pound. Tons of the stuff, yes carloads of it, were sold to handloaders around the country. However, this was not canister powder — where every lot has the same burning characteristics. Different lots of this 4895 varied in burning rates from that similar to 3031 to that which was somewhat slower than 4064 — or about what canister 4895 burns like today. Because of this difference in burning rates, whenever a load of surplus 4895 was listed, it was customary to show the lot number so that the reader had some idea of the burning rate. Lot 27277 was fairly snappy, about like 3031.

The first deer I killed using the 405-grain jacketed bullet was again a nice, chunky doe. I was hunting with a friend, Al Horton. We had worked until 2:00 A.M. and left for the deer woods at five. It was a rather warm day, just above freezing, no wind and a warm sun. About two in the afternoon I was standing on a granite boulder surveying the woods when I heard a slight noise behind me. Wheeling, I spotted a doe that had come in from behind and was now angling away toward the laurel thickets. Swinging around, I put the Redfield Sourdough directly behind the ribs and pressed the trigger just as the deer made a jump. She piled up on her head between two large boulders, her hind feet kicking in the air.

Investigation showed that the bullet had smashed the last two ribs on the left side where it entered, then went northeast through the lungs and out the right side of the neck. From there it went through a three-inch maple sapling and on into an old stump — all in a straight line! That's the kind of bullet performance I like! And while the Gould bullet was an excellent killer on deer, it was by no means a brush bullet due to its fragile structure.

Over the years I've read and heard a lot of comments relative to bullets in the brush, comments that give the high velocity bullets the nod, and others that give the heavy modest velocity bullets the nod. For myself, I'll put it this way: All bullets are subject to deflection in the brush, some less than others. Of course, velocity is a factor as is bullet structure and bullet weight. But if we can accept the fact that a 25-grain bullet from the .17 Remington at 4,040 fps is the poorest, and that a 500-grain full jacket at 2,040 fps from the .458 Winchester (or possibly a 500-grain bullet at 2,700 fps from the .460 Weatherby) is the best with an appreciable difference between the two, then it stands to reason that all other calibers must lie somewhere between those extremes.

The 400 or 405-grain jacketed bullet from the .45-70 at a velocity of a shade over 1,800 fps is an extremely dependable killer on just about any game on the North American continent. Muzzle energy for a bullet of that weight and speed is a bit over 3,000 foot-pounds. And despite the fact that where you hit them is far more important than what you hit them with, there are many times that the latter means the difference in whether you get the deer or whether it makes off to die in the brush.

The first day of doe season in 1959 was bitter cold with almost four inches of powdery snow on the ground. Betty was carrying the Winchester 1886 .45-70 with 400-grain Barnes bullets (the exposed lead filed off to make a flat nose) loaded with our standard menu of 53 grains of 3031.

About nine o'clock Betty headed out toward a ridge, knowing that I'd swing a circle, coming up in front of her. Now although Betty was a good rifle shot and could easily handle the .45-70, she was not an experienced hunter. Sure, she had hunted with me for a few years, but deer hunting is something where you can spend a lifetime and still be in the learning curve. However, after giving her time to get positioned on the low ridge (or bench as we called it), I made a semicircle through an old slashing, approaching her stand from the south.

I was about two-thirds of the way through my little drive when I heard the unmistakable bellow of the .45-70. I stopped and waited a few minutes, thinking that if there was more than one deer, the others might double back and run into me. Then I heard a second shot and figured it was the *coup de grâce*, and I resumed working slowly toward her.

Three minutes later I heard a third shot, this time further away. And minutes later a fourth shot still further yet. I thought she had crippled one and had gone after it.

I was still working slowly toward her position on the ridge when I crossed a blood trail and, just off to my right, saw a large doe piled up in the snow. Through the trees I could see that the blood trail led from the ridge where Betty had been standing. At first I was confused, but then the picture became clear. In her inexperience my wife thought she had missed the first deer because it turned and ran even though she had made a perfect heart shot. On the second deer, her shot was too far back.

That was the only time in over fifty years of hunting that I ever tagged a deer I hadn't personally shot. But I wasn't about to leave it in the woods and my wife's action had been perfectly normal for one who didn't realize that a heart-shot deer often wheels and runs.

By the time I finished gutting out, Betty had her deer secured, though some distance from me, and we began dragging them out. It was more than a mile-and-a-half to home, some of it uphill. At one spot the trail led up a very steep pitch underneath two fallen trees that were about four feet above the trail. I dragged my deer up the pitch and then went back to help Betty. Though that was thirty years ago, I can see her face yet as she told me, "I shot this deer and I'll drag it out!" She did; all the way to the house.

But the point is that even though she made a poor shot on the second deer, she was able to follow it down within a short time. The heavy .45-70 bullet not only left a good blood trail, but sickened the animal so much that it was incapable of flight. This is the whole point of the big bores. However much we like to place the bullet exactly right, sometimes it doesn't happen, and in those cases you need all the extra wallop you can get.

The only time I ever saw a .45-70 fail to leave a blood trail was one morning when my youngest son carried the Winchester and I worked a pine patch for him trying to stir up a deer. I wasn't a third of the way through the pines when I heard Frank shoot and a few minutes later he showed me where the buck had stood when he fired. It wasn't more than thirty yards away, but there wasn't a drop of blood anywhere nor was there enough snow on the ground to follow a track.

Despite Frank's insistence, I thought he had missed, and after looking around for half an hour, I resumed hunting. I hadn't gone twenty steps when Frank found the buck piled up in the pines not thirty yards from where it had stood when he shot. The bullet had entered and exited high in the chest, pulping the lungs. But all of the blood remained in the chest cavity, none of it being pumped out to leave a trail — unless by some fluke both Frank and I missed seeing the blood trail.

7

A Question of Pressure

Sometime during the summer of 1951 I met Henry M. Stebbins, an accomplished gun writer with several books under his belt. Henry, or Harry as he preferred to be called, was very conservative in his reloading as well as his thinking, and despite our age difference (or maybe because of it), we became fast friends. We did a lot of shooting together, some hunting, hours and hours of talking, and my family and I shared many Sunday chicken dinners cooked Southern style as only Glenn Stebbins could cook them.

Harry Stebbins had a beautiful Remington rolling block, originally owned by his father, chambered for the Sharps .40-50 bottleneck with the $1^{11}/_{16}$-inch case. This little rifle sported one of the first Lyman tang sights, personally installed by William Lyman. Harry was proud of that rifle and many were the afternoons that we spent shooting a 260-grain cast bullet backed by whatever amount of black powder Harry could get in those reformed .45-70 cases.

One of those afternoons I showed up with the Winchester 1886 .45-70 and several rounds of ammo loaded with the Gould bullet and 54 grains of 4895 (lot 27277). Harry was a small man physically and the big Winchester belted him around quite a bit. Finally he asked me what load I was using, and when I told him, his face paled.

As I said, Harry was very conservative — a prudent

characteristic for a handloader — and he insisted that the load was downright dangerous and begged me not to use it again until he wrote to Tom Florich, who worked closely with Phil Sharpe and others on the staff of the *American Rifleman*. I agreed to this despite the fact that the November 1950 issue of the *Rifleman* indicated that pressures with that load averaged about 29,000 psi as tested in the H. P. White Laboratories.

While Harry was writing to Florich, I wrote to P. O. Ackley, Elmer Keith and to the Winchester Repeating Arms Company. The varied opinions on this load that exist today, existed then as well. Winchester responded with a telegram followed by a letter warning me of the load's dangers. Parker O. Ackley assured me that the action would lock up long before I could get any really dangerous loads in it, and Elmer Keith considered the load as standard for any 1886 Winchester .45-70.

As for Tom Florich, although I don't have his original letter, as I recall he made a remark somewhat to the effect that I couldn't get enough 3031 in the .45-70 case and still seat a bullet to the proper depth to be dangerous. I continued to use 53 grains of 3031, or 54 grains of 4895, with the Gould bullet and 400-grain or 405-grain jacketed bullets.

Looking back on it, I have to agree that Harry Stebbins' concern was somewhat justified. In those days all of the .45-70 cases available had the old style protruding primer pocket which made for a weak case at the juncture of the rim and case body. More than that, there were still a lot of old military cases and commercial cases around that at one time had been fired with a mercuric primer. As most of us know today, mercury ruins a brass case to the extent that it readily comes apart if it is reloaded.

On the other hand, it is really quite difficult to work up high pressures in a straight case as long as you use a powder of reasonable burning rate and a bullet of a weight compatible with the cartridge. The inside of a modern, solid head .45-70 case is $1^{15}/_{16}$ inches deep. If the bullet is seated a half-inch deep, and many bullets are seated deeper, this leaves a combustion chamber within the case only $1^{7}/_{16}$ inches long. In short then, once the bullet has moved a full $1\frac{7}{16}$ inches from its seated position, the volume of the combustion chamber has doubled. This is in sharp contrast to most bottlenecked cartridges like the .30-06, .270, 7mm and others where the bullet must move down the barrel several inches before the volume of the combustion chamber is doubled. And the slower the volume of the combustion chamber is increased, the faster and the higher is the pressure increase.

This is not to say that you can poke any load you want in any .45-70 chamber you want and get away with it. You can't; some rifles just aren't strong enough. It is merely mentioned to point out that with reasonable loads using reasonable powders and reasonable bullets, the .45-70 is generally a low to moderate pressure cartridge. Even the DuPont *Handloader's Guide* dated January 1977 lists a load of 51.5 grains of 3031 with a 405-grain bullet as giving an average velocity of 1,795 fps with 27,000 CUP (copper units of pressure). And this little publication doesn't even make a distinction as to which rifles the load can be used in, thus implying (incorrectly, I believe) that it is safe in all rifles.

8

Multiple Bullet Load

One time on a visit with Charlie, I picked up one of his .45 Colt moulds for a 250-grain bullet. He told me this particular mould cast a bit big for the pistol and that maybe the bullet would work for light loads in the .45-70. It did cast big, about .457-inch, and I had some degree of success with light charges of fast-burning powders. However, since I really had no use for such a load at that time, my experimental desires bent in a different direction.

I have forgotten now exactly what load I used, perhaps about 20 grains of 4759 or some light charge of 4227, but I found that with such a charge I could seat one of Charlie's .45-caliber pistol bullets completely within the case and a second bullet on top to its normal seating depth. The inside bullet was seated on top of the powder without crushing any of it, and the second bullet at normal depth made the cartridge look perfectly normal. At fifty yards this little tandem-bullet cartridge shot great, the bullets striking about two inches apart.

I've long forgotten who I put my exhibition on for, but under the pretext of showing how well the .45-70 shot, I made a big fuss about putting up a clean target at fifty yards. I fired one shot, and when we checked the target there was a pair of snake eyes just straddling the center. My friend chewed on his lower lip a bit as he studied the target, but said nothing.

Another shot and another pair of snake eyes in the same

general location. My friend counted out the holes with the tip of his finger and then looked at me.

"What the hell," he asked, "is going on?"

I never used the load for anything, but it certainly had its possibilities.

Although I switched to the .375 H&H for all of my deer hunting for about 23 years, I still carried on an affair with the .45-70 as it is one of the most versatile cartridges in existence. It is not a long-range hunting cartridge unless one is very good at estimating range and the proper lead on running deer. At ranges over 125 yards, 150 yards at the most, the trajectory of the bullet is such that a misjudgment of range by as little as twenty-five yards can cause a total miss. And at ranges as short as fifty yards a misjudgment in lead at a fast running deer can cause a total miss or, worse yet, a gut shot. Any way you slice it, the .45-70 is at its best at ranges up to seventy-five yards in thickets of pine, laurel and hemlock.

While such limitations have little appeal to the younger hunters, the fact remains that most big game is killed at ranges of less than one hundred yards, and much of it less than fifty. In over fifty years of hunting, I've shot but one deer at a range of over 150 yards, that with the .30-06 using Jack O'Connor's favorite load of 52 grains of 4320 behind a 150-grain Remington bronze-point bullet.

If you are capable of judging the range, and I guess some people are, then the .45-70 is plenty accurate and a good killer at any of the sensible ranges at which a man ought to be shooting. I recall once when my brother Ernie and I were out plinking, I noticed a piece of board about 8 x 12 inches nailed to an old line-fence hemlock some thirty or forty years previously. It was a 175 or 200-yard shot, yet by holding the width of the square bead on my Redfield Sourdough above the top edge, I was able to dump half a dozen shots into the board with no trouble. The problem is that when you are hunting, you seldom take the time to make an accurate judgment of range, if indeed you think of it at all.

Getting back to lead on running game, it takes a 400-grain bullet at a muzzle velocity of 1,800 fps about .086 second to travel fifty yards, while a deer running at 25 mph covers a bit over three feet in the same length of time. Thus, if you forget your lead and aim at the chest, you are likely to spoil some steaks or miss the deer altogether.

9

Looking for a Single Shot

Although I was using the .375 H&H for much of my shooting beginning the mid-1950s, I still had a good single shot .45-70 in the back of my mind and even went so far as to start designing an action for a double rifle chambered for the old cartridge. Naturally, this was one of those dreams that we often have, but which seldom comes true, even though in the late 1880s there were a few double-barreled .45-70s manufactured.

I continued to read every article on the .45-70 I could find, including Keith's "Pumpkin Rolling with Accuracy" that showed up in two different issues of the *American Rifleman*. I made tallow wads by melting tallow in boiling water, letting it cool and then taking the resultant sheet off the top of the water. This was used in my black powder loads for the Springfield Trapdoor.

My trapdoor carbine had a long, hard trigger pull and, not knowing any better, I tried to correct it by filing down the amount of sear engagement on the tumbler. If I had taken it to Charlie, he would have pressed a pin in the full-cock notch on the tumbler, thus limiting the amount of sear engagement to the thickness of the sear. But by filing things down the way I did, unless I put a lot of pressure on the trigger, the sear would slip into the half-cock notch when the trigger was pulled. Since I wasn't all that happy with the Springfield to begin with, I sold it for the same $10.00 I had paid for it.

Then I purchased a Winchester Hi-Wall single-shot in .32-40 with a good octagon barrel thinking that I would rebarrel that to .45-70. But with a growing family, that was another project that never materialized and the .32-40 was sold without my ever having fired it.

Somewhere along the line Harry Stebbins showed up at the house one rainy day with a beautiful sidehammer Sharps having a heavy, octagon barrel chambered for the .44-77. Harry also had several boxes of original factory ammunition loaded with pater patched bullets, and we drove down into a field along Mallory Run and spent the afternoon sitting in his station wagon shooting at rocks on the far edge of the creek. In the rain, the black powder smoke hung like a cloud and sometimes we had to wait until things cleared up before we could resume shooting. I've wondered many times since just how many dollar bills we burned up that afternoon by shooting all that original factory ammunition. The last time I saw that Sharps rifle, the barrel had been removed and was in a lathe being turned round and cut back to twenty-four inches to make it easier to carry! People who do things like that should be hung!

Bill Ruger was the man who finally came to my rescue. In fact, Bill Ruger is the man who put single-shot rifles back in the deer woods. In 1971 I acquired one of his No. 1 Tropical rifles chambered for the .375 H&H to replace the Winchester Model 70 I'd been using since the 1950s. The Ruger was shorter and easier to handle. However, by 1974 I was beginning to feel the weight of a heavy rifle and started looking for something lighter in a caliber that offered a lot of smash.

The little Ruger No. 3 chambered for the .45-70 is one of the sweetest woods rifles a man will ever carry. It is short, lightweight and powerful with the extent of the latter being determined only by how much recoil one can handle. At about 6½ pounds, the No. 3 is a bearcat when you start shooting a 400-grain bullet in the 1,800 fps bracket. Nor is this the limit of the velocity to which the heavy bullet can be driven from the Ruger.

It has long been my opinion that because of the strength of the Ruger single-shot action and the potential of the .45-70 cartridge when specially loaded for that action, that the cartridge designation on the barrel should be ".458 Ruger" or some other unique designation to distinguish it from the .45-70. There is no comparison between the garden variety .45-70 cartridges and those which can be loaded for the Ruger No. 1 or No. 3.

The Ruger No. 3 .45-70 complete with Weaver K3-W scope, Lyman 48LEE receiver sight and a Perry Ammo Sling holding three cartridges. This little outfit is probably the best brush hunting rig the author has ever used. *(Photo by Frank M. Matthews)*

Close-up of the Perry Ammo Sling on the buttstock of the Ruger No. 3. The cartridges are loaded with the Hornady 350-grain bullet backed by 55 grains of 3031. The author never carried more than three cartridges in the ammo sling because it upset the rifle's balance.

10

The Two Rugers

When I first got my Ruger No. 3 .45-70, scope blocks for that model were hard to come by, so that fall I continued to carry my .375 with the exception of the second day of the season. That morning I struck out with the No. 3 and its factory open iron sights. The rifle was a dream to carry, but my old eyeballs just couldn't do the job with the bead-type front sight and little "U" or "V" notches in the rear sight. A few years later Harold Reynolds made me a $\frac{1}{8}$-inch blade front sight and, by removing the elevation slide from the Lyman No. 16 folding rear sight to expose a deep "U" notch $\frac{3}{16}$-inch wide, I had a sighting combination that I could use for fifty or seventy-five-yard shooting. In fact, I have this combination on all of my hunting rifles including my flintlock, and in some cases have filed the top of the rear sight to put the bullet exactly where I want it.

At any rate, for the first one or two years that I had the No. 3, I did not carry it deer hunting other than that one day because of a lack of good sighting equipment. After I was able to get a set of Weaver scope blocks, I mounted a spare Weaver K6 scope on the rifle and started working with it.

Up until about the mid-1980s all of the Ruger single shots that I ever saw had considerable freebore ahead of the chamber. This was new to most of us, and some people didn't like it because it was not conducive to good accuracy with standard length cartridges. To get the best from a chamber with freebore, you have to seat the bullets out to fill the gap. Personally, I liked the idea because it resulted in greater case capacity (if you really wanted to use it) and it usually precluded the use of the ammunition in some other rifle that was weaker than the Ruger. Further, as I found out later, the freebore was made to order for paper patched bullets.

However, the freebore had its drawbacks, too. Where I had used the Gould bullet with good accuracy in the Winchester, I could not do the same in the Ruger unless I seated the bullet out so far that the forward grease groove was fully exposed. More than that, the barrel on my No. 3 would not permit driving the soft cast bullets much over 1,400 or 1,500 fps with any degree of accuracy. Whether this was due to shallower rifling or a somewhat rougher barrel in the Ruger, or maybe the freebore itself, I don't know. I do know that a change in bullet moulds was required and in time I purchased three RCBS moulds with the 300, 400 and 500-grain cavities.

At first though, I stuck to jacketed bullets in the No. 3 powered by my old standard charge of 53 grains of 3031. Even though recoil was fearsome, this load using the K6 scope would gnaw a large hole in the target at 100 yards with every bullet cutting the hole left by its predecessor. When I used the Hornady 350-grain roundnose bullet, I used 55 grains of 3031, and with the Hornady 300-grain I used 56 grains of 4198. However, neither of the lighter bullets shot as well as the heavy 400-grain jacketed bullet.

On the day before Thanksgiving in 1976 I acquired my Ruger No. 1 .45-70. This was a beautifully stocked rifle and handled like a dream. It had what I call "pointability"; that is, it shot where you looked. And though I didn't have much time to work with it, I carried it the following Monday for the opening day of deer season. I had mounted a Weaver K3 scope on it, and was using the Hornady 350-grain bullet backed by 55 grains of 3031, the same load I was using in the No. 3.

On the second day of the season, at 1:15 P.M., I topped a rise in the middle of a field and spotted a buck quartering away from me at about 135 yards. He wasn't running hard and I put the crosshairs on the leading edge of his chest and touched it off. The buck never flinched and within seconds was out of sight in the woods.

I trailed that buck for about a hundred yards before finding the first speck of blood and one or two long white hairs. The buck was gut shot, very low and far back. For the next three hours a friend and I stayed on his trail, now clearly marked with heavy splotches of blood where he fell and sprinkles where he walked.

About ten minutes before dark we came upon the buck lying down in a thicket of thorn apple. The bullet had grazed his belly just ahead of the hind legs. A half-inch lower would have meant a clean miss.

Turning this data over in my mind, I felt that I wanted higher velocity from the 350-grain bullet. I particularly liked the Hornady 350-grain roundnose because I felt it was a good compromise between the high explosive nature of the 300-grain hollowpoint and the deep penetration qualities of the 405-grain bullet. Further, its jacket was light enough to assure good expansion without the fragmentation of the hollow point.

Because of its solid rubber recoil pad, the No. 1 Ruger is far easier to handle with heavy recoil than the No. 3, so by the time the next deer season came around I was using the Hornady 350-grain bullet backed by 55 grains of 4198. This is a considerably more potent load, and although I have never chronographed it, Bob Hagel clocked it from a Ruger No. 1 at 2,195 fps. From my No. 1, accuracy was somewhat better at the higher velocity than it had been from the earlier load.

My chance to try this load on deer came about four o'clock in the afternoon in about the same spot where I'd shot the buck the year before. I had been walking most of the day, and by late afternoon was totally pooped. I sat down on an old bale of hay that someone had conveniently left along the uphill edge of the field. I hadn't been there five minutes when looking out across an adjoining field I could see five or six doe running directly toward me. There was a fence between us, and I watched them through the scope as they jumped the fence and headed up the slope at a slight angle to me. All the time I watched them, I kept telling myself, "They are farther away than they look through the scope. Hold your fire until they get close."

It didn't do any good. They were at least a hundred yards away when I fired the first shot at which they turned broadside and barreled full tilt across my front. Quickly reloading, I put the crosshairs on the chest of a big doe and pressed the trigger. She went down in a heap with a smashed pelvic bone and a few ruined steaks off the top round.

A Lyman No. 16 folding leaf rear sight from which the elevation slide has been removed. When used in conjunction with a ⅛-inch blade front sight, this makes an excellent open iron sight combination for close-in brush shooting.

Close-up of the left side of the Ruger No. 3 .45-70 showing the Lyman 48LEE receiver sight nestled beneath the Weaver K3-W scope.

(Photo by Frank M. Matthews)

11

More Deer with the No. 1

Both of the foregoing incidents show only too clearly that if you are going to hunt deer with the .45-70, you should stick to the woods where ranges are usually short, and you should be a good judge of lead and range. In the first case, I hadn't led the buck far enough nor had I held high enough. In the second case, due to the excitement of fast action, I hadn't led the doe at all, and if I had been using the slower load that I used on the buck, the odds are that I never would have touched her.

Still, I don't think the lesson had fully sunk home. I felt that a better-shaped 350-grain bullet would help a lot and I ordered 400 semi-spitzer bullets of 350-grain weight from Randy Brooks of Barnes Bullets. Foolishly I also requested a .049-inch jacket.

These bullets were plenty accurate, though I had to seat them way out in order to fill the freebore of the chamber. This left a lot of air space in the case with the 56-grain load of 4198, so I switched to 63 grains of 3031. Again, I didn't have access to a chronograph at the time, but I would guess that velocity remained about the same. The one important thing worth noting is that the rifle usually performed its best with a load that gave 100 percent loading density; that is, no air space between the powder and bullet.

Because of the heavy jacket on the Barnes bullets, I never

did use them on deer, but before another season I decided to try the Hornady 300-grain hollowpoint backed with 56 grains of 4198. This load is approaching 2,300 fps, and right away I learned that my Ruger No. 1 showed a strong preference for the lighter bullet. Accuracy was a bit better than with the 350-grain bullet.

This time it was a nice fat antlerless buck that got in the way. I heard him coming, coming fast, and by the time I had him spotted he was trotting at an angle through heavy brush. I swung with him and the instant I saw clean hair in the scope, I pressed the trigger. That was the same time that a two-inch diameter hickory chose to get in the way. I hit it dead-center, and when the rifle settled from recoil I could no longer see the deer. He was stretched out on the ground ten feet away from the sapling.

How close that buck had been to the hickory when I fired, I'll never know. An autopsy indicated that one large piece of bullet about the size of a nickel and six or eight smaller fragments had pierced the hide going in, and one large fragment was found on the off-side under the hide. No part of the bullet exited.

Despite its splendid performance — and if you don't believe it was good performance, try the same stunt with a high-velocity rifle — I believe that had the bullet been a 350-grain roundnose, it would not have fragmented on the hickory and would have totally penetrated the buck. I also believe that a 300-grain bullet shaped like the 350-grain Hornady would have done the same thing, maybe even better. I wrote to Joyce Hornady about this, sending him a photo of the section of hickory splintered by his bullet, but was unable to convince him of the need for a change in bullet shape or a new bullet.

Barnes Bullets offered exactly the bullet I wanted, a 300-grain roundnose with $\frac{1}{32}$-inch pure copper jacket, and I ordered 400. While waiting for them, I went back to the Hornady 350-grainer backed by 55 grains of 4198.

The new Barnes bullets didn't arrive until the second day of the next deer season. When I came in from hunting that night, the bullets were waiting for me, the prettiest .45-70 bullets I had ever seen. My nephew, Joe Piccolo, was there for supper that evening and when I remarked that I was going to load up some of the new bullets for the next day, he questioned the advisability of carrying them in the woods without putting them on a target first. I assured him that there couldn't possibly be any problem as I already had a good load for a 300-grain bullet and no sight setting change was required. I was happy as a lark and anxious to poke a deer with the new projectile.

Fortunately I didn't have the opportunity. The following Sunday with a break in the deer season, I put the Ruger on the sandbags and tried the 300-grain Barnes bullet. To say that I was stunned was the understatement of the year. The bullet would barely stay on a dinner plate at a hundred yards.

The following evening when I returned from deer hunting, I called Randy Brooks, and had my answer. His 300-grain bullet, from the set of dies he was working with at the time, had less than a caliber of bearing surface. Coupled with the freebore of the Ruger, there was no way they would ever shoot. Randy told me he intended to have a new set of dies made to correct the problem.

With the failure of the 300-grain Barnes bullet, I continued to use the Hornady 350-grainer and later that season made the kind of shot I wanted. The deer was facing me at a slight angle and the bullet struck on the left side of the neck traveling lengthwise through the body and coming to rest under the hide on the backside of the right hind leg. The recovered bullet weighed 331 grains (a little over five percent weight loss) and measured $^{13}/_{16}$-inch across. That is pretty good performance in any man's book. The next season I shot another deer with that same bullet and load, but have forgotten the particulars other than the fact that it was a one-shot kill.

Section of the hickory tree that got in the way of a 300-grain Hornady bullet backed by 56 grains of 4198. The hickory is a shade over two inches in diameter. The bullet and fragments of the bullet went on to kill an antlerless buck on the far side of the tree.

(Photo by Frank M. Matthews)

Expanded 350-grain Hornady bullet recovered after traveling lengthwise through a deer. The recovered weight is 331 grains (5 percent weight loss) and the expanded diameter is $\tfrac{13}{16}$-inch. Load was 55 grains of 4198.

12

Back to the Ruger No. 3

Despite my success with the Ruger No. 1 .45-70, I liked my little No. 3 the best. It was lighter to carry and was far less finicky about what load was stuffed in the chamber. Whereas the No. 1 favored a 300-grain bullet, the No. 3 showed no particular preference, but shot them all equally well and a shade better than the No. 1. However, I wanted to carry the No. 3 as an iron-sighted rifle and, as yet, didn't have the sighting system I wanted.

I finally had a riflesmith fit a Lyman 66A to the receiver of the No. 3. The sight was not made for that rifle and although it was usable, it was a cobbled up job at best. It did, however, let me use the rifle as I wanted and I soon replaced the front sight with an eighth-inch blade sight that Harold Reynolds made for me. By covering the face of the blade sight with orange fluorescent tape, I could see to shoot almost as early in the morning or late in the afternoon as with a scope. I was happy with the system except that I would rather have had a quality receiver sight made especially for that rifle.

Such a sight wasn't long in coming. One day while having a cool one with Charlie Canoll, the sight became a topic of conversation. Within minutes he was poking around boxes of items that had been on his shelves when he closed his gunsmithing establishment in 1957. Charlie came up with a brand new Lyman 48LEE receiver sight that, when put alongside the No. 3 receiver, fitted it exactly. From that point on, it was only a matter of time before Charlie had drilled two new holes in the 48LEE base to match the holes I already had in the receiver, and within minutes my little No. 3 had a top quality receiver sight. What made it even better was that when I slid the staff to its lowest position, I could mount a Weaver K3-W over the peep.

Although there is no question that a scope sight is the best sighting system ever devised, I won't carry a rifle in the woods that doesn't have a set of good iron sights sighted in with the ammunition I'm using. All too many times during the Pennsylvania deer season I've had to hunt in a steady rain or heavy snow when a scope is all but useless. And many times after such a day of hunting, I've talked to others who relied solely on their scope and found water in the tube come nightfall. During foul weather I like to be able to take a scope completely off the rifle and continue hunting with iron sights. I don't want an offset scope that clears the iron sights, nor do I want a set of those see-through mounts; both are an invitation to a cookie-cutter gash over the eyebrow when you lower your head to use the iron sights with the scope still in position.

With the Lyman 48 and the Lyman 66 you can push a release button on the rear of the sight to permit rapid adjustment or removal of the sight staff. This is an excellent feature for the man like myself who uses both light and heavy loads in the same rifle. Because of the relationship between barrel time and recoil of the .45-70, loads involving various weight bullets and/or different velocities usually impact a considerable distance apart, thus requiring two different sight settings.

To facilitate changing from one setting to another, I sight in the rifle with one load and then attach a narrow strip of fluorescent orange tape across the staff and base. Then with a razor blade, I cut through the tape between the staff and base. From that point on, I never touch the adjustment knob nor do I ever worry about a certain number of "clicks"; I merely slide the sight staff up or down until the ends of the tape are aligned and the rifle is sighted in. I sometimes have settings for two different loads indicated on my sight in this fashion.

13

Search for a Cast Bullet

Until the early 1980s I used jacketed bullets for hunting, strongly favoring the Hornady 350-grain bullet as the best compromise. Since I was looking at retirement in a few years, I started stockpiling bullets, powder and primers to tide me through those years. I had always purchased bullets as I needed them and, as I recall, the Hornady 350-grainer was going for about $8.50 for a box of fifty. This wasn't too bad, but when inflation caught up with the bullet market — just as I started stockpiling — the price shot up to $13.50. This was more than I had paid Randy Brooks a few years before for the special semi-spitzer 350-grain Barnes bullets, and it was just too much for my wallet. I switched to cast bullets.

As mentioned earlier, the Gould hollowpoint did not deliver the accuracy from the Rugers that it did from the Winchester, perhaps because of the freebore ahead of the chamber. Further, neither of my Rugers would handle cast bullets of a soft alloy like 16 to 1 tin and lead to any degree of accuracy, whereas in the Winchester this was no problem. About the softest bullet I could drive in the 1,800 fps bracket from the Rugers was a gas check bullet having a hardness of at least 9 Bhn as measured on the LBT bullet hardness tester. Even with a hardness factor this low, expansion is an iffy thing. (Incidentally, if you go in for cast bullet hunting, you should certainly have a bullet hardness tester.)

While the .45-70 ranks supreme in the cast bullet hunting field, and proper bullet placement is the most important factor relative to killing power, the fact remains there is no substitute for reliable expansion if the bullet doesn't go exactly where you want it to go. And here we are talking about a matter of one or two inches — not half a foot.

In 1983 both of my sons were home to join me in deer hunting. Frank was going to use my iron-sighted Ruger No. 1 while George carried his own rifle, a Ruger Model 77 .30-06. I was carrying my No. 3 .45-70.

I had spent the entire summer working on cast bullet loads for the .45-70s. In the No. 1 the load consisted of a 312-grain bullet (about 9 to 10 Bhn) cast from an RCBS 45-300-FN mould backed by 32 grains of 2400 powder and fired by a Large Rifle Magnum primer. This load gave an average velocity of 1,711 fps. For the No. 3 I was using a 345-grain bullet from an Old West mould (again 9 to 10 Bhn) driven by 33 grains of 2400 and fired by a Magnum primer. This load averaged 1,746 fps over the Oehler 33D Chronotach with Skyscreens.

I wasn't totally satisfied with either load. While they both gave good accuracy, I questioned whether either of the bullets would give any or adequate expansion. In fact, I advised Frank that he should pass up any attempt at a neck shot; that he had to put the bullet in the chest area, preferably where it would smash bones.

Naturally, on the afternoon of the first day Frank spotted a nine-point buck feeding about thirty yards away and the only shot he could take was a neck shot. He passed it up. Going back to the same area the following day, sure enough, about three in the afternoon that buck came into the area feeding in the same general spot. This time the buck turned broadside on, giving Frank the shot he wanted. The buck wheeled and bolted down a steep wooded hillside to a creek bottom where he piled up in a pool of water.

The bullet actually struck a bit low in the brisket, taking off the lower tip of the heart and shattering the foreleg on the off-side. When I say shattered, I mean just that. A piece of leg bone two inches long was thrown completely free of the animal, and other fragments of bone were driven into the chest and lungs. The wound caused a massive hemorrhage, putting the animal out of commission in less than a minute.

I am not certain whether there was any expansion to that bullet or whether the bone fragments acted as secondary projectiles. But if it was the latter, what might have been the outcome if the bullet had been three inches further back and three inches higher, through the lungs without touching the heart or the heavy arteries attached to the heart? My guess is that the deer would have run considerably further with a lot less blood trail, and in dry woods this can make tracking very difficult.

When hunting deer I am fully committed to having a bullet that gives rapid expansion, plus deep enough penetration to reach the vitals on an on-end shot. The 350-grain Hornady bullet delivered such performance and I believe the same performance could be derived from a cast bullet.

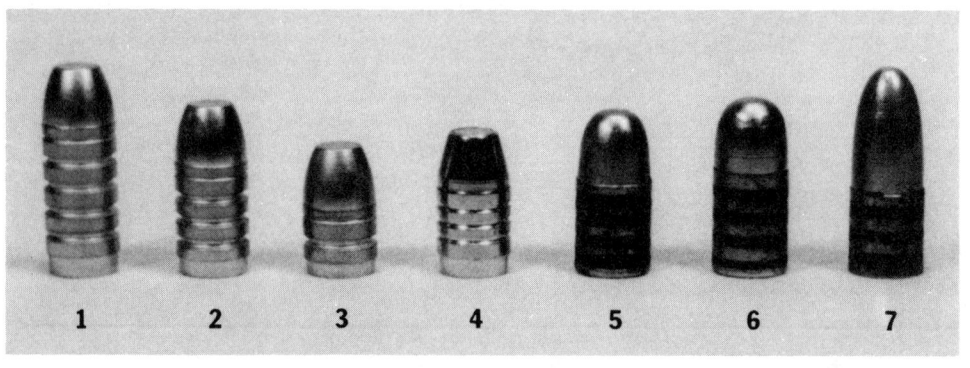

Cast bullets used in the Ruger single-shot rifles. From left to right: *1)* RCBS 45-500-FN, *2)* RCBS 45-400-FN, *3)* RCBS 45-300-FN, *4)* Old West .459-350, *5)* Lyman 457483, *6)* NEI 430.458GC and *7)* the Lyman Postell 457132 shortened by one base band. *(Photo by Frank M. Matthews)*

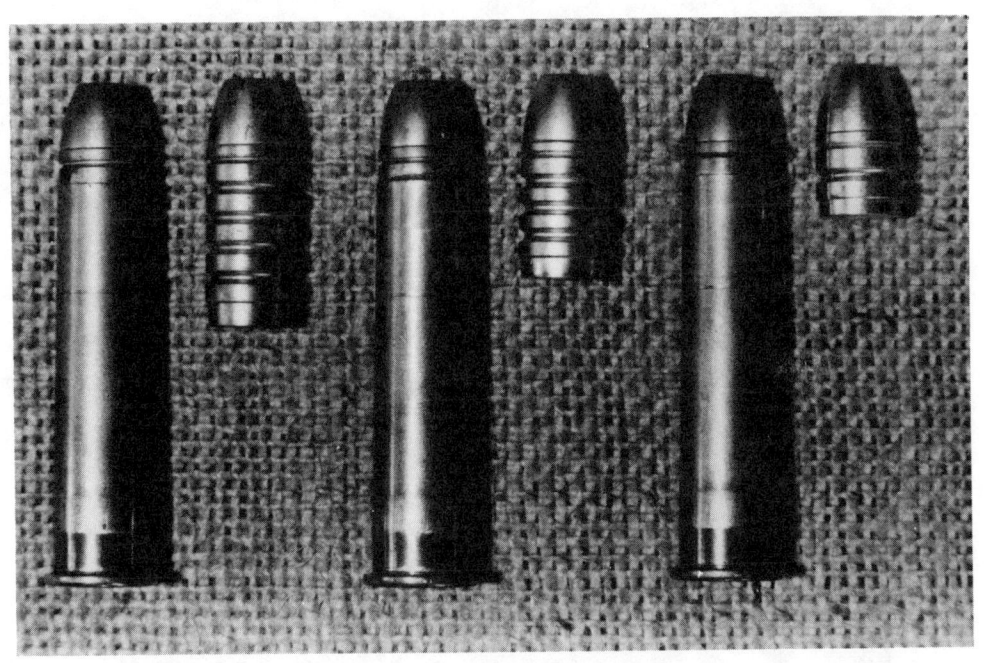

These are the three RCBS bullets shown alongside a cartridge loaded with each respective bullet. Note that the overall length of the cartridge is the same regardless of which bullet is used. This can be vitally important when selecting a bullet mould for the Marlin 1895 in which the overall cartridge length is limited. *(Photo by Frank M. Matthews)*

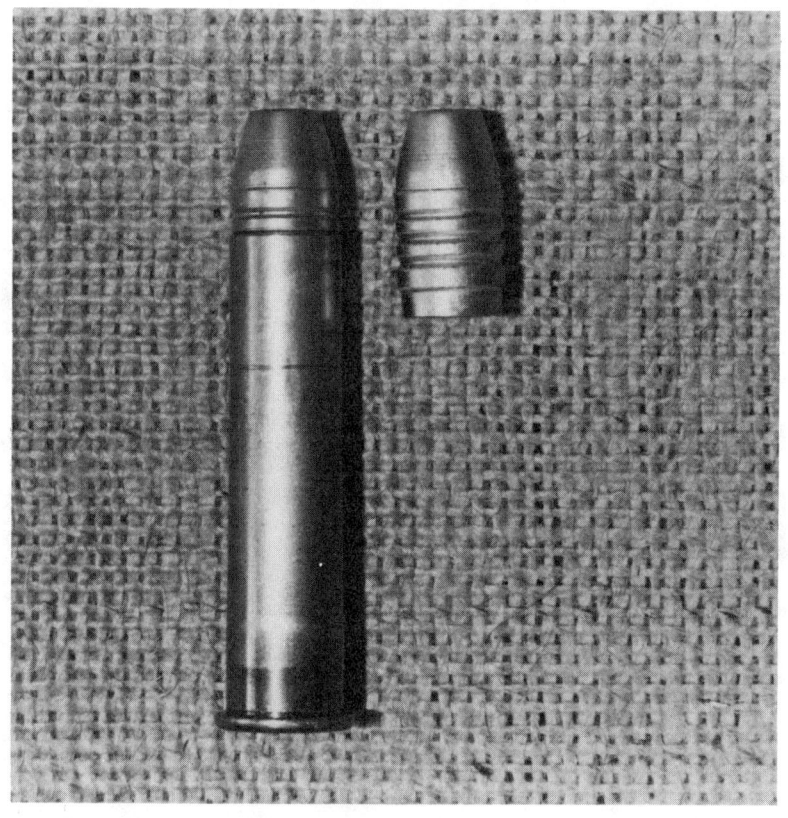

Old West bullet .459-350 beside a loaded cartridge. This bullet was exceptionally accurate when freshly loaded with 55 grains of IMR-3031. However, the author could never determine why accuracy deteriorated within a few days of loading. *(Photo by Frank M. Matthews)*

14

RCBS, Old West and Hoch Moulds

I mentioned earlier that when I acquired my Ruger .45-70 rifles, I also purchased the three RCBS bullet moulds. When cast of Linotype metal, bullets from these moulds weigh 300, 400 and 500 grains. Softer alloys produce bullets ranging from 20 grains heavier for the smallest mould up to 30 grains heavier for the big bullet.

All three of the RCBS bullets are excellent in the .45-70, though the heaviest bullet is seated quite far back in the case when all the grease grooves are covered. The nose shape is identical on the three bullets with the weight being added to the back end in the form of more driving bands. All of the bullets sport a gas check shank for the crimp-on gas check.

Since I was so well-satisfied with the 350-grain Hornady bullet, I wanted the same weight in a cast bullet and would have had it if RCBS had seen fit to add one more driving band to the 300-grain bullet. They were not about to do this.

The Old West bullet moulds made by Ken Chapman, then of Grand Junction, Colorado, had just the bullet I wanted. It was catalogued as No. 460-350GC, but is stamped 459-350. This bullet was especially designed for the new Marlin 1895 rifles and the Winchester 1886, and had a truncated cone nose and a gas check shank for crimp-on gas checks. The mould itself is double-cavity, made of brass with three large $3/16$-inch diameter dowel pins to assure alignment. The mould is an example of superb craftsmanship coupled with excellent bullet design.

In my Ruger No. 3, when backed with 55 grains of 3031, the Old West bullet gave outstanding accuracy at 100 yards, groups that ran between 1 and 1½ inches *when the cartridges were freshly loaded.* Let the cartridges stand for three or four days and groups spread to four to six inches. What caused this, I was never able to find out, and I did everything to correct it including a heavy crimp, tighter neck plug and Magnum primers. Nothing helped, though I'm convinced to this day that the problem is in the load and not the bullet. However, that is why the load that I used with the Old West bullet the years my sons hunted with me was 33 grains of 2400 instead of my usual heavy load of 3031.

My next move was to send Richard Hoch one of my Old West bullets and have a nose-pour mould made for the same shape bullet, but just slightly heavier, 355 grains when cast of 75 percent wheelweights and 25 percent lead. Bullets from the Old West mould weighed about 345 grains when cast of this alloy. I also told Hoch that I wanted wide, shallow, flat-bottomed grease grooves instead of the narrow grooves cut on a radius. Whether or not this was a mistake, I don't know, but I have always preferred such grease grooves on my bullets.

A Hoch nose-pour bullet mould is a study in perfection. The heavy top and bottom plates are held in parallel with a rugged, large diameter spacer and swing on a common pivot screw. Bullets are round when they come from the mould and drop from the cavity of their own weight or with a very slight tap. Most important, bullet bases are glass-smooth and square with the axis of the bullet.

Just as I ordered, my new Hoch bullet weighed 355 grains, and the best load I found for it was 44 grains of 4198 fired by a Remington 9½ primer. This gave an average muzzle velocity of 1,818 fps and was very accurate.

On the first morning of the buck season that year, the temperature stood at about 60 degrees when I left the house. About an hour later a cold front roared through the area and the mercury plummeted into the 20s. I had dressed fairly warm but not warm enough. At noon, when a buck ran across my front in some fairly open woods about thirty yards off, raising the little No. 3 seemed like a frozen, slow-motion effort. I got the shot off all right and even though it seemed that the sights lay just right, the buck gave no indication of a hit. Nor could I find any sign of hair or blood, though I covered the area thoroughly for the next two to three hours.

To this day I am not certain whether I hit that buck or not, though I have a haunting fear that my bullet was too far back, too high and that it gave no expansion. I had to have something better.

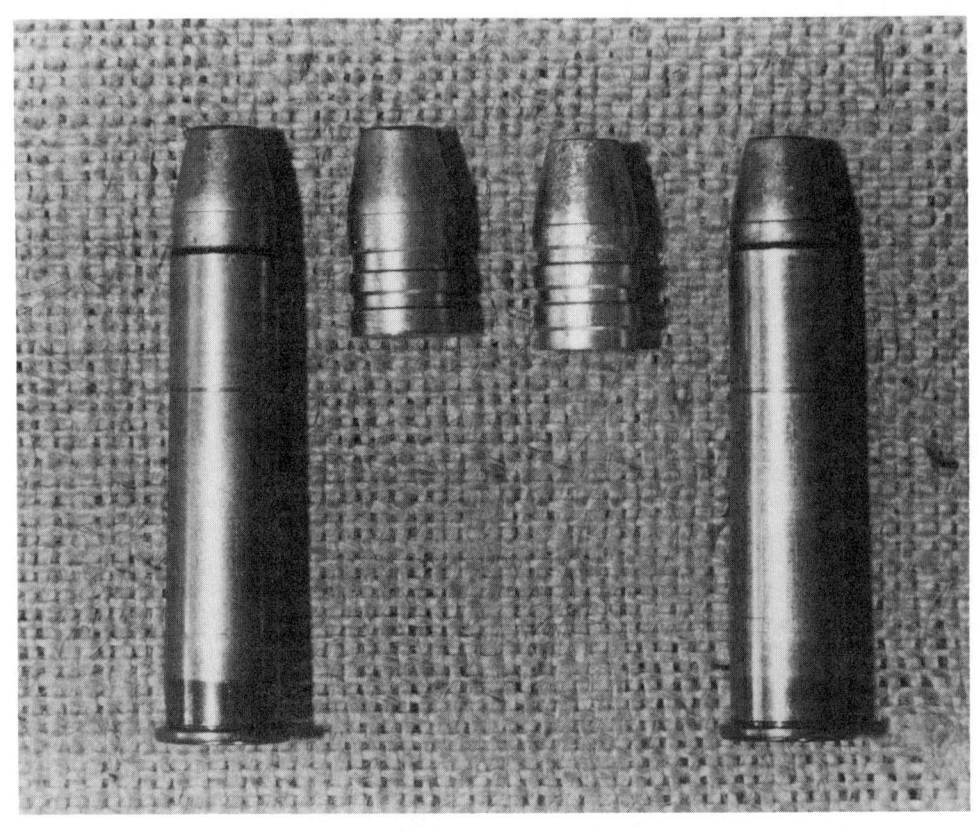

Two bullets from moulds made by Richard Hoch. Both bullets weigh 355 grains when cast of an alloy consisting of 75 percent wheelweights and 25 percent lead. The bullet on the left is a plain base, while the one on the right is a gas check design made especially for deer hunting. *(Photo by Frank M. Matthews)*

The two Hoch bullets. Note the glass-smooth bases. This is the way the base of a cast bullet should be in order to obtain the best accuracy.
(Photo by Frank M. Matthews)

15

Paper Patched Bullets

Around 1981 Charlie Canoll made me a nose-pour, adjustable bullet mould to cast a cupped-base, smooth-sided paper patched bullet for the .45-70. It was a dead ringer in shape to the old Sharps paper patched bullet, and would cast bullets ranging in weight from about 325 to 565 grains. The body diameter was .450-inch, just as I had requested.

This was not my introduction to paper patched bullets. I had made a mould of my .375 H&H back in the 1950s and had done enough experimental work to learn that such a bullet had a lot of potential, but was more time-consuming to prepare than a grooved, lubricated bullet. However, since it was evident that I couldn't drive a *soft* grooved lubricated bullet at the velocities I wanted from my Ruger .45-70s, the paper patched bullet was the last resort.

Before I get into what I did with paper patched bullets, you have to think of a paper patched bullet as a *paper-jacketed bullet*. That's exactly what it is. All the paper does is prevent the bullet from leading the barrel and build up the diameter of the bullet to its proper size to prevent gas leakage. It's as simple as that. You should also understand that a *soft* paper patched bullet (or any other bullet, for that matter) when in the rifle barrel is caught between opposing forces, the powder gases at the rear of the bullet pushing it toward the muzzle, and the inertia (weight of the bullet), barrel friction and air resistance (column of air within the barrel) all working to hold the bullet back. A soft bullet being caught between these forces has a tendency to squash outward, filling the grooves of the barrel and thus gripping the rifling, perhaps more tightly than a hard-cast grooved, lubricated bullet.

The first paper patched bullets I started to work with in the .45-70 were cast of pure lead and weighed 355 grains. I patched these with a 16-pound bond paper having 25 percent cotton fiber content, and loaded them in front of 55 grains of 3031 and fired by a Remington 9½ primer. The very first group I shot at one hundred yards measured 1^{15}/$_{16}$-inch horizontally by ⅜-inch vertically! And this load would consistently group within two inches, sometimes hovering close to the inch mark. Later I increased the bullet weight to 363 grains using the same charge for an average velocity of 1,945 fps. Accuracy remained the same. Even though I still had many problems ahead, I knew I had arrived!

My problems were in lack of versatility. It seemed that I could not load any paper patched bullet with a light or moderate load and get decent accuracy, nor could I obtain the kind of accuracy I wanted from a bullet of 400 grains or heavier. More than that, if I hardened the bullets with so little as 3 percent tin which I thought would help in the accuracy department, the patch would strip in the barrel and the barrel would be severely leaded.

This problem was finally traced back to the diameter of the unpatched bullet and the fact that smokeless powder burns differently than black. Thus, it does not bump a bullet up in the barrel quite the same way that black powder does.

Measuring the inside of my rifle barrels showed that the groove diameter (across the bottom of the grooves) was .458, while the bore diameter (across the top of the lands) was .4515, or .0015 inch larger than my unpatched bullet.

To correct this condition, I asked Harold Reynolds to make me a hand swaging die, or "bumping up" die, to increase the diameter of my bullets to .452. This was no problem for a master mechanic and graduate engineer, and within a day or so I had a die that worked perfectly. I had to grease the bullets very lightly when I put them in the die, then tap the base plunger once or twice with a four-ounce plastic hammer to bring the bullets up to size.

Bumping these bullets up just .002 solved all my problems. Of course I had to go to a thinner onionskin paper to compensate for the larger diameter bullet, but that was no hardship. The thinner patch is easier to apply to the bullet.

By using a paper patched bullet whose unpatched diameter is equal to or slightly larger than the bore diameter of the rifle lets one use either hard or soft bullets at a very wide velocity range. It worked so well that I later had Dave Farmer, who bought out the Hoch bullet mould business, make me another paper patched bullet mould that cast a .452-inch bullet. By using that mould I didn't have to go through the bumping-up process.

Before continuing, I should mention that this bullet diameter information is very important. I later purchased a Ruger No. 1 chambered for the .458 Winchester Magnum and, because its bore was slightly tighter than my .45-70s, it much preferred the .450 diameter bullet over the .452.

At any rate, I was now in business with a bullet that I could make at home, that would shoot as good as any jacketed bullet I could buy and that would give me needed expansion. All I had to do now was to try it out on game.

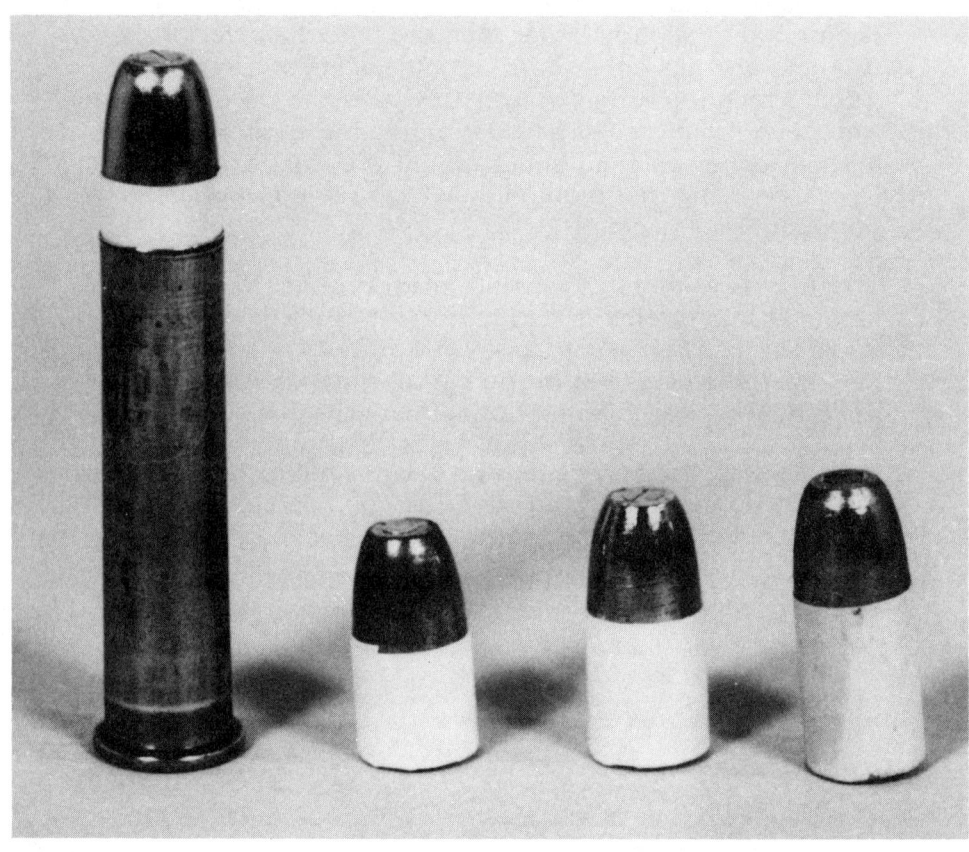

A .45-70 cartridge loaded with a paper patched bullet alongside three other paper patched bullets. Note the patch on the bullet at the left is improperly applied; it is uneven at the top.

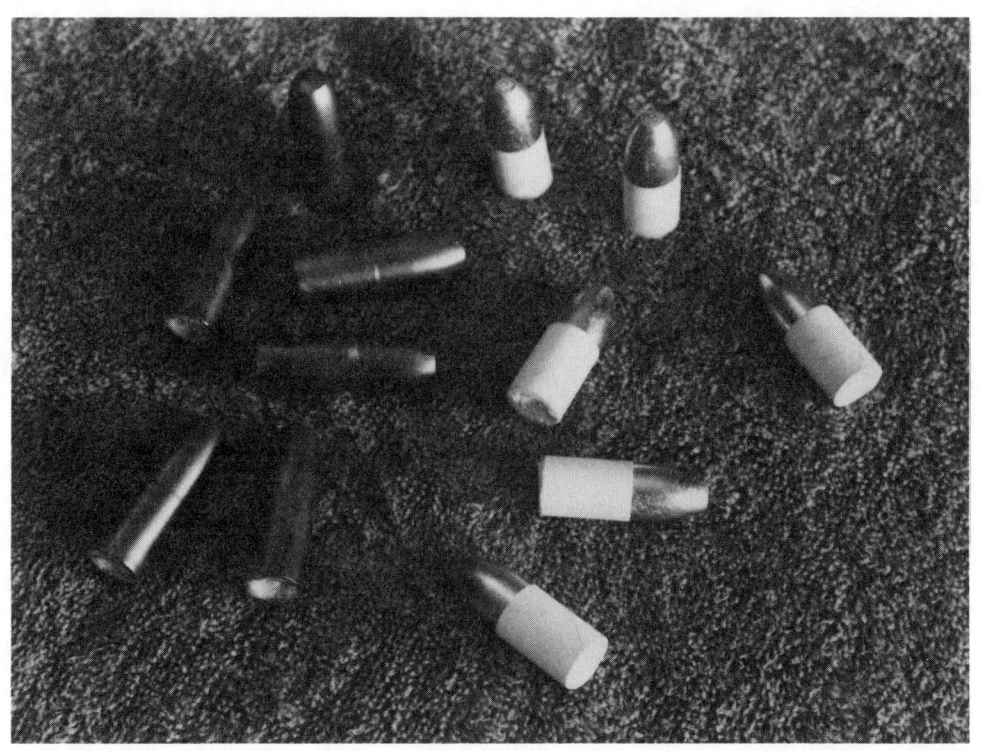

Paper patched bullets for use in the Ruger .45-70. The bullets with white patches are from the Dave Farmer mould; the darker bullets are from a mould cut by Charlie Canoll. The darker bullets have been waterproofed by "cooking" them in beeswax for ten minutes then rubbing them with powdered graphite after they had dried.

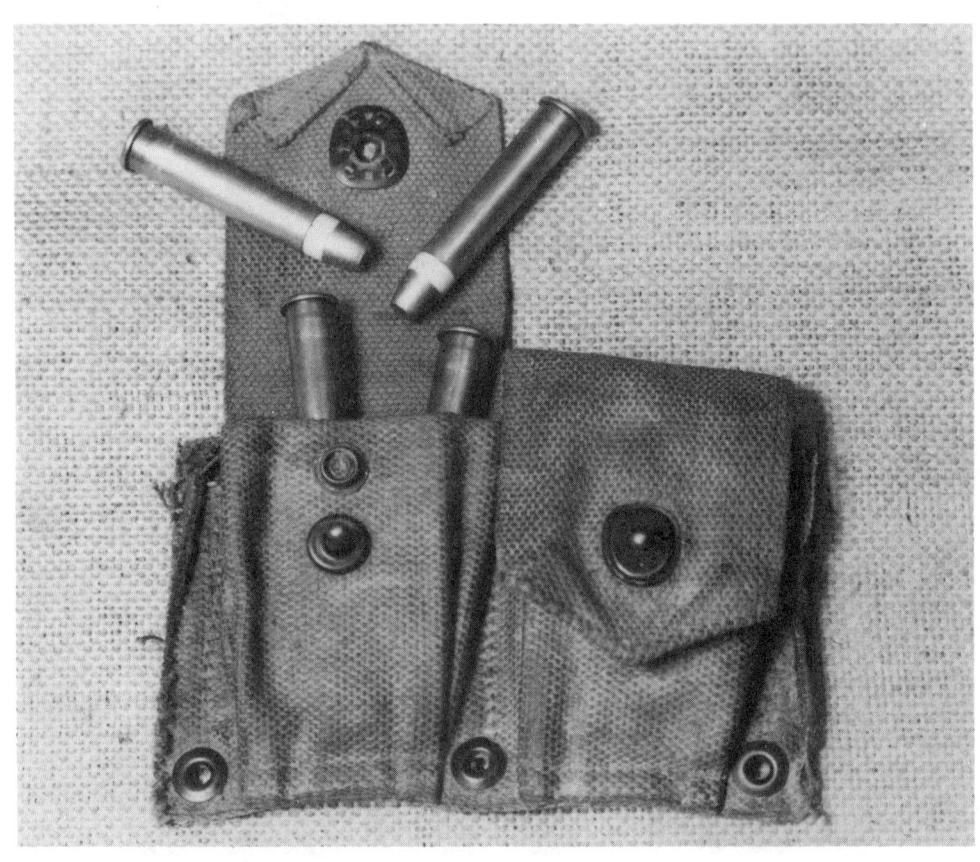

After switching to paper patched bullets, the author removed the Perry Ammo Sling from the buttstock of the No. 3 and now carries his spare cartridges in a pair of pockets cut from an old bandolier belt. The pockets have been waterproofed by impregnating the fabric with a mixture of beeswax and Vaseline.

The author at his shooting bench test-firing a .458 Magnum loaded with 550-grain paper patched bullets. This rifle handles paper patched and cast bullets exceptionally well.

16

Deer and Wild Boar

Using paper patched bullets changed the performance of my Ruger No. 1 completely. Where previously it had never quite matched the No. 3 in flexibility of loads or accuracy, now it was equal in every respect. Further, it pointed better than the No. 3 despite its lack of a good iron sight system. Since I was planning an early season bear hunt in the Adirondacks, I set about correcting the sight problem.

Ken Ramage, then vice president of Lyman, had told me that many Ruger owners were using the new Lyman 66U receiver sight on the Ruger No. 3s. I purchased one of these and although it would fit the No. 1, the sight staff had to be raised excessively high to clear the quarter rib. To get around this, I asked Fred Cornell to build an adapter that attached to the quarter rib. I thus mounted the Lyman 66U on the adapter. Then I had Fred make a $\frac{1}{8}$-inch blade sight for up front. Now I was all set.

I went to the Adirondacks with Clyde Shipman, as fine a man and as good a hunter as one could hope for. We pitched our tent in a downpour and it rained or drizzled all three days we were there. Both of us were carrying Ruger No. 1 .45-70s and using 385-grain soft paper patched bullets (lead with 3 percent tin) backed with 53 grains of 3031. To make a long story short, we hadn't hunted half an hour when I had a shot at a nice bear at something less than thirty yards — and missed it clean! The second famous miss of my career. Oh, I've had some other misses, but nothing that smarted like the Adirondack bear or the doe that was lying down when I shot.

However, I did redeem myself that deer season by shooting the buck described in the first paragraph of Chapter 1. The 385-grain paper patched bullet struck low on the left side of the neck, ranging upward and back through the heart, lungs and heavy spinal bones between the shoulders, to come to rest under the hide on the off-side up near the back. In all, the bullet penetrated about 18 inches of muscle and bone. It mushroomed out to $15/16$-inch diameter and lost only nine grains, or about 2 percent, of its weight. The buck dropped in its tracks and was dead by the time I got to it. That's the kind of performance I was after!

One swallow doesn't make a spring — or a drunkard. And so I wanted to try the paper patched bullets on something else, something heavier and meaner than a whitetail deer. In April of 1988 my brother Allan and I went to Chestnut Hunting Lodge at Taylorsville, North Carolina, to hunt wild boar or, more correctly, wild hogs. Jerry Rushing was the top honcho of this outfit and had two very able men (Jack Simms and Eli Tarlton) helping us out while we were there.

Both Allan and I were using Ruger No. 3 .45-70s with paper patched bullets, my load being a 405-grain bullet with 53 grains of 3031, and Allan's load being a 389-grain bullet with 51 grains of 3031. It was necessary to use a shorter bullet with a little less powder in Allan's rifle because his did not have the freebored chamber like mine; consequently his bullet had to be seated deeper.

This is probably as good a place as any to point out that paper patched bullets should be seated so that they just kiss the rifling when the cartridge is chambered. That is, I like to see indentations of the rifling leade on the leading edge of the patch, but I don't want a cartridge rammed into the rifling so far or severely that it leaves the bullet stuck in the barrel when you eject a loaded cartridge. If the paper patched bullet is properly lubricated, seating the bullet $1/16$-inch shy of the rifling does little harm to accuracy. For lubricant, I use a mixture of 45 percent beeswax and 55 percent clear Vaseline. A thin film of this on the patch, especially at the leading edge, facilitates seating the bullet and also helps to keep the patch intact during its initial engagement with the rifling. I don't put any lube on the base of the bullet to avoid contaminating the powder.

Getting back to the boar hunt. For those who have never hunted boar, they are mean and tough to kill, often taking more lead than a whitetail. Of ten wild boar for which I have records, only three were stopped in their tracks by one shot. One of these was a small 40-pounder shot on the island of Java by my nephew, Joe Piccolo, using a Heckler & Koch semiauto in .308 Winchester with 180-grain Federal ammunition. Joe also shot four other boars, one a 220-pounder that required four shots.

The other two one-shot drop-in-their-track kills were made by my brother and me at Chestnut Hunting Lodge using .45-70s with paper patched bullets.

My hog weighed between 180 and 200 pounds. He was an old hog, old enough that the meat was rank and the sausage strong enough to walk by itself. Jack Simms had taken me in tow and pointed through the hardwoods at the big boar lying down. At first I couldn't see the animal, just a black log. And then the log got to its feet and barreled off down the mountainside. A few minutes later, for some unknown reason, the boar came back up the mountain, headed for a clearing about fifty yards away. The .45-70 was ready and I pressed the trigger the instant the crosshairs settled over the foreleg. The boar crumpled in a heap.

Now I had shot boar earlier in Tennessee and I had seen other boars shot, and just because a boar goes down, doesn't mean he's finished. Sometimes they "come back to life" dirt-mean and intent on revenge. Jack Simms and I approached this boar warily, with my rifle loaded and ready for another shot.

At twenty feet, Jack pitched a rock that struck the boar in the head. No reaction. So we advanced closer and Jack poked it under the tail with a stick. The boar was dead, the heavy paper patched bullet having pulped the lungs and passing through the chest cavity just under the spine.

Allan's shot was almost a duplicate of mine except that his bullet was enough higher to shatter the spine. Like my boar, his also was dead by the time he got to it.

That fall I shot another doe using my Ruger No. 1 and a 410 grain paper patched bullet. The bullet struck low on the left side of the neck, angled back through the heart, clipping the last six ribs on the off-side before emerging from the flank. The doe made one jump, landing on top of a brush pile where she was stretched out like a wet dishrag when I reached her. Range was about 75 yards.

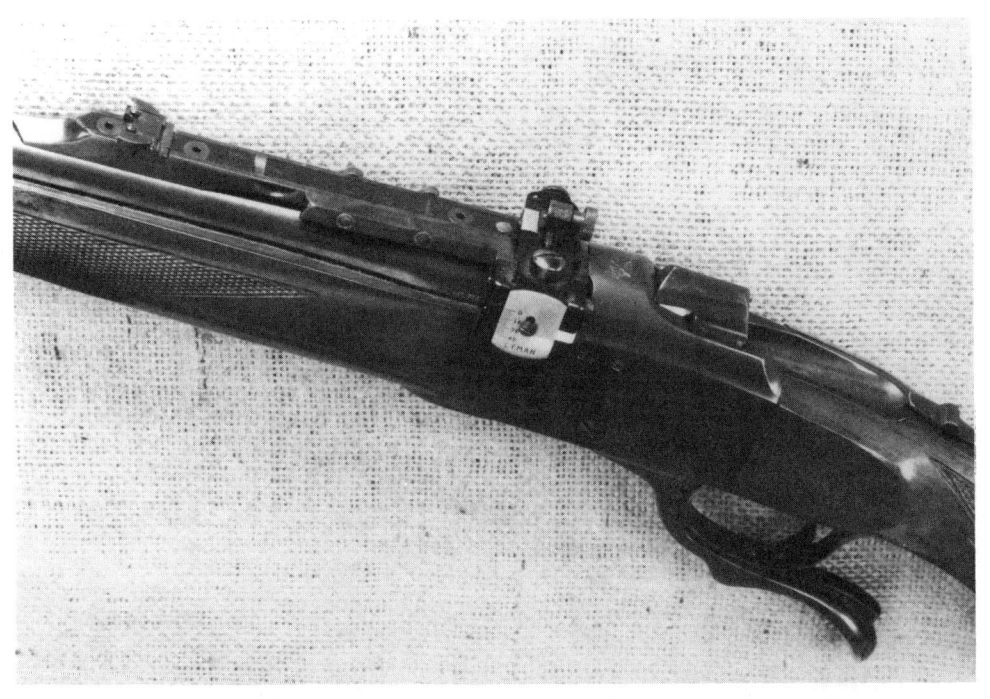

Close-up of the Ruger No. 1 with the sight adapter and Lyman 66U receiver sight attached to the quarter rib. This makes a very fast handling, accurate outfit for any normal range at which the .45-70 is likely to be used. *(Photo by Frank M. Matthews)*

This is the sight adapter with the Lyman 66U receiver sight designed by the author for mounting on the quarter rib of a Ruger No. 1 single-shot rifle. *(Photo by Frank M. Matthews)*

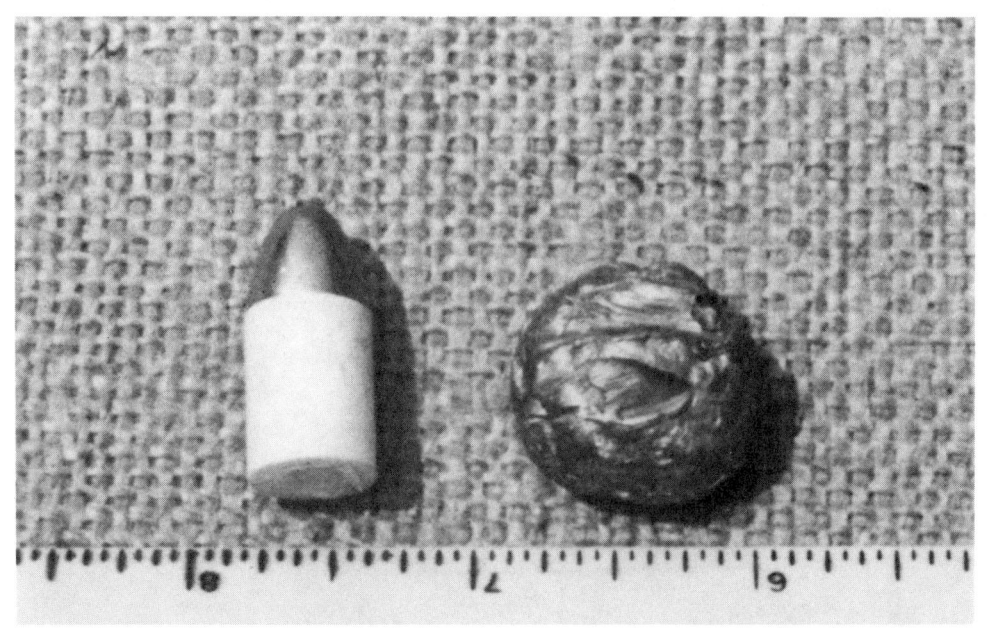

A 358-grain paper patched bullet recovered from a buck deer killed in 1987. The bullet penetrated 18 inches of muscle and bone, and expanded out to $^{15}/_{16}$ inch in diameter. Recovered weight was 376 grains (2 percent weight loss). The load was 53 grains of 3031 and the alloy was pure lead with 3 percent tin.

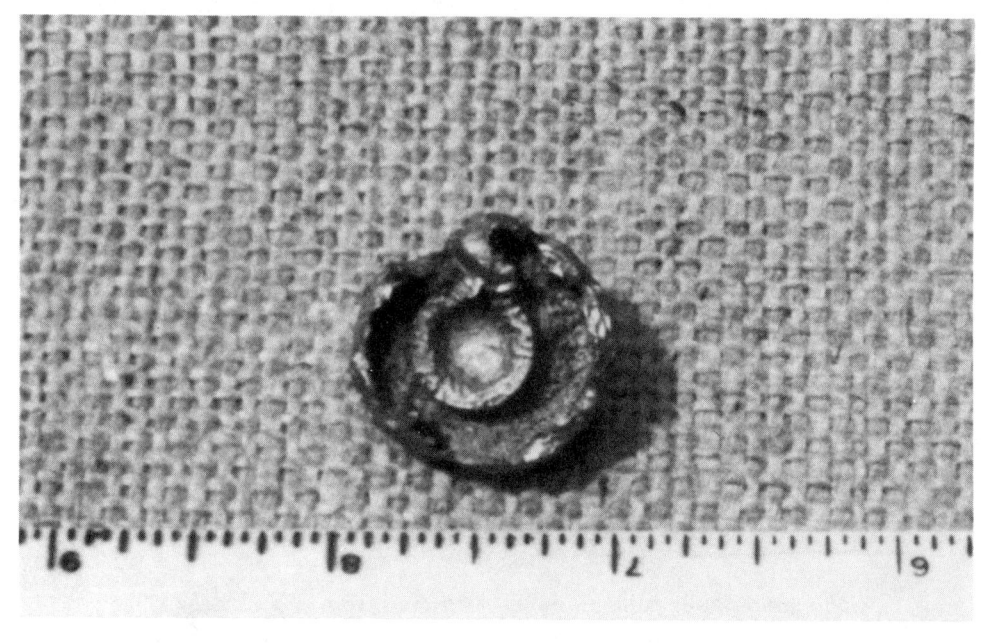

A look at the base of the 385-grain paper patched bullet taken from a buck. Note the powder marks around the rim of the base cavity.

Allan H. Matthews with a wild boar he shot with a Ruger No. 3 .45-70 at Chestnut Hunting Lodge, North Carolina. Allan used a 389-grain paper patched bullet backed with 51 grains of 3031. The boar dropped in its tracks with one shot. *(Photo by Frank M. Matthews)*

Close-up of the author's boar shot April 6, 1988, at Chestnut Hunting Lodge, North Carolina. *(Photo by Frank M. Matthews)*

17

Patching Grooved Bullets

As far as I'm concerned, the paper patched bullet is the ultimate in hunting bullets, especially in the more modest velocity calibers. A lead-tin alloy with only 3 percent tin gives the bullet just enough firmness to resist deformation from handling and loading, yet it in no way hampers expansion, nor does it contribute to bullet breakup. I have used paper patched bullets in the .30-30, .30-40, .375 Winchester, .37 Rimmed, .375 H&H, .45-70 and the .458 Winchester Magnum, and in everything except the .45 calibers, I've pushed these soft bullets between 2,200 and 2,300 fps with good accuracy.

Once I had convinced myself that the paper patched bullet was the way to go, I began giving consideration to all the bullet moulds I had on hand for grooved lubricated bullets. Was there any way these could be used in the paper patched system? There was; and it works pretty well, too! Anyone who has a bullet mould for a grooved, lubricated .45-70 bullet, plain base or gas check, has the makings for a paper patched bullet.

In my first attempts at patching grooved bullets, I merely ran the unpatched bullet through my .458-inch SAECO die and patched it with nine-pound onionskin paper. This works as long as the chamber will accept the oversize bullet, but often a ring of paper is left at the front of the chamber after firing, thus preventing a fresh cartridge from being chambered.

After putting up with this for a while, I started lubricating my patched bullets and running them through the SAECO die a second time. This irons the patch to a hard finish, pressing some of the lube into the patch. It also eliminates a lot of loading and chambering problems, and grooved bullets so patched and sized work well.

In the end, I purchased one of Dave Corbin's fine reducing dies that would allow me to resize my cast bullets from .459 or .460 down to .452-inch. Although the Corbin die might seem expensive, it costs less than two-thirds of the cost of a custom cupped-base, adjustable paper patch mould. And it allows me to use every .45-caliber grooved mould I've got as a paper patched bullet!

Before running my bullets through this die, I lubricate them with a light case-sizing lube. Because the bullets are usually quite soft, I press them through nose-first to avoid any distortion which could unbalance the bullet. But base-first or nose-first, the bullets go through the Corbin die concentrically and are then ready to be patched.

I have used grooved bullets having a gas check shank both with and without the gas check and can't determine at this stage that there is much performance difference. Whenever I choose to use the gas check, I anneal the gas check with a propane torch before applying it to the bullet and running it through the Corbin die. The annealing process takes all of the spring-back out of the gas check so that it remains tight on the bullet shank after passing through the Corbin die.

One particular grooved bullet that I used as a paper patched bullet to some extent, was the Postell bullet cast of a soft alloy so that it weighed a full 475 grains. Because the nose diameter of this bullet measures about .441 or .442-inch, I used a 1¼-inch wide patch extending it well forward of the front rotating band. This brought the nose diameter of the patched section up to .449 and provided a short bore-riding section to help align the bullet in the barrel.

Loading some of these bullets on top of 60 grains of 4064 for an average velocity of 1,772 fps, I tried them in my No. 1 Ruger. Recoil was sufficient to get my attention, but the load shot well enough to indicate that if I wanted a real bear load, this one certainly deserved further consideration. Muzzle energy for that load is 3,300 foot-pounds.

Although I much prefer using my smooth-sided, cupped-base bullets for paper patching, at one time or another I tried all of my grooved bullets and found that they worked very well. I wouldn't feel neglected if that was all I had.

18

Other Moulds and Loads

Despite the fact that I consider the paper patched bullet to be the very best in the hunting field, there are a couple of other grooved bullets for the .45-70 that deserve mention. In 1979 I purchased a mould from NEI (Northeast Industrial Inc.) for its 430.458GC. This bullet is shaped much like the Lyman 458483 but is slightly heavier with a few dimensions better suited for accuracy. The driving bands of the NEI bullet are $\frac{1}{32}$-inch wider than the Lyman bullet, and the nose diameter is .450 as compared to .444 for the Lyman. This promotes better alignment of the bullet in the barrel.

I have used the "NEI Smasher" as I call it, quite a bit, with loads ranging all the way from 29 grains of 4759 to 53 grains of 3031. While it may not deliver what you call outstanding accuracy, it is a consistently accurate bullet with almost any reasonable load. If I were to select a grooved lubricated bullet for heavy game, the NEI Smasher would be it.

Another good NEI bullet for the .45-70 is the 405.458GC. This is one of the few cast bullets with a spitzer point that will give good accuracy out of a barrel with a .458-inch groove diameter. The same bullet from my Navy Arms rolling block did not deliver good accuracy because of a much smaller groove diameter.

Weather permitting, I like to shoot my little No. 3 .45-70 every day, usually offhand at 50 yards. For this purpose I like a rather light, accurate load and, since it requires a special sight setting, I want a bullet that will transmit the maximum energy or shock for the velocity involved. I'm interested in the transmission of energy because I often carry this rifle with me for a walk in the woods and I don't care to use heavier ammunition that makes more noise and requires a different sight setting.

For a long time my load for this purpose was the RCBS 45-300-FN bullet backed by 10 grains of Unique and fired by a Large Pistol primer. This gives an average velocity of 940 fps and is very accurate for 50-yard shooting, or even 75 yards. Accuracy can be improved upon by using a Dacron filler between the powder and base of the bullet.

While the RCBS bullet does an excellent job, it really didn't satisfy me for two reasons: First, it is a gas check design and I didn't need a gas check at 940 fps. Contrary to what I have read, gas check bullets without gas checks do not give *consistently* good accuracy. Second, even though the RCBS is a flatnosed bullet, the meplat or flat area is not large enough to transfer the maximum amount of energy derived from that modest load. I wanted a bullet that was almost a true cylinder, like a full wadcutter.

Charlie Canoll made a mould for just such a bullet. I call it my Utility Bullet because I use it for my target, plinking and woods walking load. The bullet weighs a bit over 300 grains and even at such a modest velocity as 940 fps is equal to or better in killing power than any load one would use in a .45 Long Colt.

The nose diameter of my bullet measures .453 which would be too large to chamber in a rifle with no freebore. It would also probably work very nicely in a Marlin 1895 having a Micro-Groove barrel with its very shallow rifling, but if I were having a special mould cut for a rifle that didn't have the freebore, I would reduce the nose diameter to .450-inch.

Over the years I have read many times about using the .45-70 as a small game rifle, usually with a few grains of Bullseye powder and a roundball or a "collar button" bullet like the old Lyman No. 457130. Such a load greatly increases the versatility of the rifle and gives the advantage of a lot more practice in the field, something that none of us can get too much of.

However, as promising as this sounds, there are problems involved that don't surface until you are actually in the field. My favorite whisper load for the .45-70 was 3.8 grains of Bullseye with a 355-grain plain base bullet from a Hoch nose-pour mould. At twenty-five yards this bullet and load *on the target range* gives squirrel head accuracy without any trouble and with no more noise than a .22 Short, though beyond twenty-five yards, accuracy deteriorates rapidly.

However, I used this load quite extensively one summer, and that fall I took it after grey squirrels. Now I've hunted small game with a rifle off and on for my entire life, and I've used the rifle exclusively for small game for the past fifteen years, so I'm really no slouch at it. But after four days of hunting with that load and firing upward of a dozen cartridges, I had one single grey squirrel that I'd tagged through the ribs when I had aimed for the head.

Almost every day I went out, I confirmed the accuracy of the load by sitting down and taking a shot at twenty-five yards, yet when it came time to shoot at game, it seemed that I couldn't make a hit.

Finally it dawned on me. The velocity of this load was only 496 fps. That meant that the bullet was in the barrel for a relatively long time after the trigger was pressed and, as such, was greatly affected by recoil or the slightest movement of the rifle. Whenever testing the load or confirming its accuracy, I was firmly seated on the ground with both elbows on my knees and an iron grip on the rifle. While hunting, I was in many different positions, often shooting offhand, and this was affecting the accuracy. Had I speeded the bullet up to 950 or 1,000 fps, I would have eliminated the problem. But then I would have had more noise than I wanted and a relatively unsafe condition when you consider the range and ricochet characteristics of a .45-caliber bullet at the higher velocity. In my book, the .45-70 is out for small game.

At the same time I was working with the small game load,

I also tried to work up a shot load for snakes, frogs or even sitting grouse. This is always difficult for a rifled barrel because the shot or shot enclosure always attempts to follow the rifling, thus throwing a donut pattern as soon as the shot emerges from the muzzle. Although able to overcome this to some degree, shot loads from the .45-70 didn't impress me all that much.

The shot load that was fairly successful for me was 10 grains of Unique fired by a Large Pistol primer. On top of the powder, I put an eighth-inch card wad made for a .410 gauge brass shell. These used to be sold by Alcan and measured .457-inch. After the wad, I made a card sleeve from a 3 × 5 file card. This encircled the inside of the case. Then I took a plastic .410 gauge shot sleeve, cut it off to fit the case capacity I had left, inserted it into the case and filled it with No. 9 shot. A thin card wad on top held in with a light crimp finished the affair.

At ten or twelve yards this will give a fairly dense pattern with no hole in the middle, but after losing two sitting grouse and a rabbit with the load, I gave it up as unreliable.

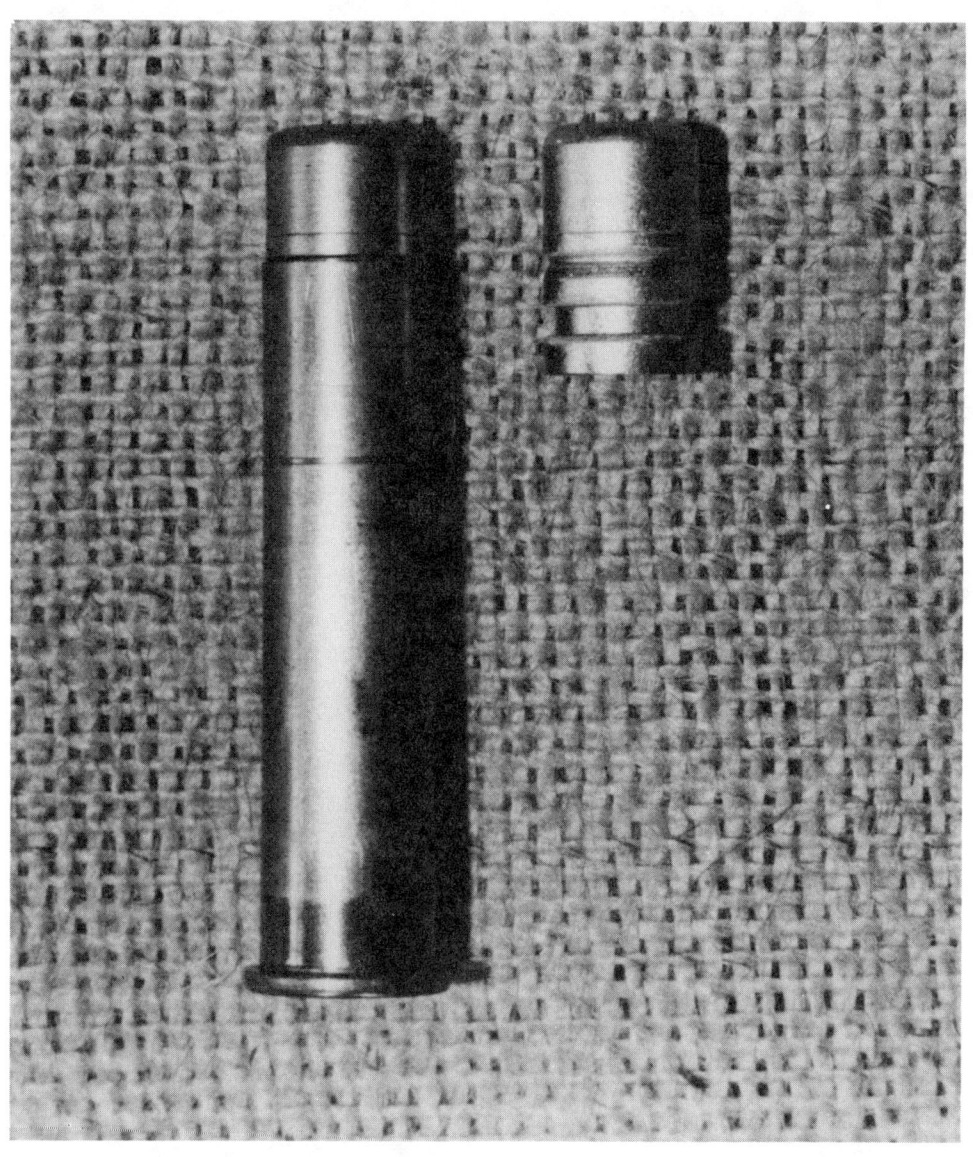

This little Utility Bullet from a mould made by Charlie Canoll is one of the best ever used by the author. When loaded with 10 grains of Unique, the bullet has an average velocity of 940 fps and is very accurate up to seventy-five yards. *(Photo by Frank M. Matthews)*

19

Powders

If I had to select any one powder for use in a Ruger .45-70, I'm not certain what that powder would be. Without question, if I were to use only heavy loads with bullets up to about 420 grains, 3031 would be the powder. It ignites easily and it burns clean, though in the straight-walled .45-70 case its complete combustion is marginal. That is, with some load combinations you will find unburned powder grains in the barrel. In fact, my 53-grain load with the 400-grain bullet fired by a Magnum primer barely burns clean. Yet on the Oehler 33D Chronotach the extreme velocity spread is only 25 fps for a standard deviation of only 10. And these figures are supported or complemented by snug grouping of the bullets out on the hundred yard mark.

With extra-heavy bullets, that is anything over 430 grains, my choice of powder for a heavy load would go to 4064, the next slowest burning of the original DuPont powders. Here again, the powder ignites easily and burns clean — barely. When I worked up the load of 60 grains of 4064 with the 475-grain paper patched Postell bullet, I started out with 55 grains and worked up. Even with a 58-grain charge, the powder was not burning clean, leaving traces of unburned powder in the barrel. However, if I were to increase my bullet weight to 530 grains, I would cut the charge to 55 grains and still get a clean burning load. I have done this in the .458 Winchester, and by using the proper width patch it can be duplicated in a strong .45-70.

With the lighter bullets, 4198 works good — the 300 and 350-grainers, and 3031 can also be used with these bullets for lower pressures, but it will not always burn cleanly. And it has been my experience that when the powder doesn't burn cleanly, you often have fliers. Whether this is due to the unburnt grains left in the barrel, erratic ignition, or a combination of both, I don't know.

One of the very best powders I have used for 1,500 and 1,600 fps loads is 4759 with a Dacron filler. In my Navy Arms rolling block, I have but two loads that I can depend upon to stay in 2½ inches or less at 100 yards with iron sights. One load uses the RCBS 45-400-FN bullet with 28 grains of 4759 and a Dacron filler, while the other uses a 550-grain paper patched bullet from my Canoll mould with 24 grains of 4759 and a Dacron filler. Velocity with either of these loads is probably well below 1,500 fps, more likely about 1,250 for the heavy bullet and 1,350 for the lighter.

In my Rugers I use 32 grains of 4759 with a 400-grain paper patched bullet and 35 grains with a 363-grain paper patched bullet, the latter load giving an average of 1,594 fps. Actually either of these loads with a soft paper patched bullet is more than adequate for deer.

Also, 4759 is my choice of powder whenever I'm going to use a priming charge with a main charge of black powder. In this function it is claimed that one grain of smokeless priming charge is the equivalent of three grains of black, and by increasing the priming charge in a barrel that is properly throated so that the bullet can be seated out, one can duplicate the old 45-100-550 with the much shorter .45-70 case. I personally think that's hiking the priming charge quite a bit, though it's apparently safe in the Rugers.

For a priming charge I like to use about 13 to 15 percent of the full, normal black powder load. That is, for the .45-70 case, based on a 70-grain charge, I use 8 to 10 grains of 4759 as my priming charge. In the .458 Winchester case, which holds a full 90 grains of black powder with room left to seat a bullet, I use 12 grains of 4759 and 72 grains of FFg black behind a 550-grain paper patched bullet for an average of 1,342 fps. This is a good accurate load developing 2,739 foot-pounds of muzzle energy.

In working up a good priming charge, I start at the usual recommended 10 percent of the normal load, working up slowly until accuracy shows a marked improvement. And it is my experience that there is usually a vast improvement in a load with a 13 to 15 percent priming charge as opposed to a load with a 10 percent. *There is also a pressure increase that should be considered when using original black powder rifles.* Under no condition would I exceed the 15 percent priming charge.

Hercules 2400 and DuPont 4227 powders are also good for loads in the 1,500 to 1,600 fps bracket, as well as for priming charges in duplex loads. In both functions I believe they are a poor second to the 4759, though a number of black powder shooters swear by 2400 to duplicate black powder loads.

As mentioned in Chapter 13, my son Frank killed a nine-point buck using the RCBS 45-300-FN bullet backed by 32 grains of 2400 for an average velocity of 1,711 fps. While this load functioned well and gave good accuracy, I believe it was near the top working limits of the 2400 powder. I also tried 33 grains of 2400 with the 345-grain Old West bullet for an average velocity of 1,746 fps and an extreme spread of only nine fps. However, on that particular test, I fired only three shots as opposed to the usual five.

I used quite a bit of 4227 in the old Winchester and it always showed a lot of promise. The loads that I worked with in the Rugers required a Dacron filler and gave fair results when so loaded.

Thirty-five grains of 4227 with Dacron behind my Hoch 355-grain bullet gave an average of 1,677 fps, while 33 grains behind a 408-grain paper patched bullet gave an average of 1,523 fps. Both of these loads showed considerable velocity spread for five shots. However, when I used these same loads with other paper patched bullets, I received good accuracy with a much-reduced velocity spread.

Thirty-five grains of 4227 behind a 328-grain paper patched bullet gave 1,689 fps, and 33 grains behind a 363-grain paper patched bullet averaged 1,542 fps. A Dacron filler was used in both cases.

When it comes to duplicating black powder loads with smokeless, Unique powder seems to do it all and do it well. I have probably used more pounds of Unique powder in my .45-70s than all the others combined, and only modest charges at that. Usually somewhere in the range of 15 to 17 grains of Unique will give good accuracy with 300 to 400-grain bullets. I always use a Large Pistol primer with Unique and never use a filler except with my Utility Bullet, a load that I spoke of earlier (Chapter 17). Sixteen grains of Unique behind the RCBS 45-300-FN bullet averages 1,352 fps with superb accuracy. This is an excellent practice load, easy to shoot and not too much noise. If I could have but one powder, Unique certainly would be a likely candidate.

Back in the 1950s when Bruce Hodgdon started filling the shelves with surplus powder, he came out with his 4350 Data powder, later known as H-4831. This stuff was offered at the unbelievably low price of $27 for a fifty-pound keg, or $49.50 for a hundred-pound keg. At these prices it was too economical to pass up, even if you didn't have a rifle to use the stuff in! Every time I took a deer hide to town, I traded it for a can or two of H-4831, and later three of us went together on a fifty-pound keg. In all I acquired about thirty pounds of this powder and used it only occasionally in the .375 H&H or the .30-06.

Then I found that a .45-70 case full of the original H-4831 with a heavy bullet shot pretty well, except that there was a trail of unburned powder grains left in the barrel. These had a bad habit of creeping back in the chamber, thus interfering with the next cartridge. Worse, these unburned powder kernels would manage to get into the works of the No. 1 and No. 3 actions and bind things up but good. Further, I often had fliers when there was unburned powder in the barrel.

The first thing that came to my mind to alleviate this condition was to use a priming charge of a faster burning powder just as I had with black. But using an ignition charge with smokeless was brand new territory, and I could recall only too well the number of articles and letters in old issues of the *American Rifleman* telling of handguns being abruptly disassembled by the so-called duplex loads of that time. It's like walking barefoot in a chicken yard and trying to keep your feet clean at the same time!

On page 71 of the NRA book *Cast Bullets*, the late Col. E. H. Harrison mentions using two grains of Unique next to the primer in a .30-06 case to help facilitate the burning of a charge of 4831 behind cast bullets. This information started me in the right direction, but instead of using Unique, I went to the slower-burning 4759 and used five grains of it along with 50 grains of H-4831. Whatever bullet I was using (at first the NEI 430.458GC), I seated on top of the powder so that the powder column was held in place and there was no mixing of the two powders.

This load shot very cleanly, but since I was shooting over snow, I could see that a considerable amount of the unburned H-4831 was merely being blown out of the barrel and that the 4759 was not functioning as a priming charge. I then replaced the 4759 with 5 grains of Unique fired by a Large Pistol primer. Again I used the NEI Smasher bullet weighing 425 grains, and the resulting average velocity was 1,547 fps. There were no unburned kernels of powder on the snow and accuracy was good.

Switching from the NEI bullet to a 400-grain paper patched bullet with the same load gave an average velocity of 1,507 fps — 40 fps *slower* than the heavy bullet. Accuracy was excellent out of my No. 3, and the velocity spread for five shots was only 35 fps. A 408-grain paper patched bullet with the same charge delivered an average velocity of 1,511 fps, again with good accuracy.

Later I tried a very soft 362-grain bullet from my Hoch plain base mould, the bullet being sized down in my Corbin die and then patched with nine-pound onionskin. Because this bullet was seated further out in the case, I increased the charge of H-4831 to 54 grains and maintained the 5-grain charge of Unique. This time the average velocity was 1,616 fps and the extreme velocity spread for five shots only 31 fps. Again, accuracy was good.

I have fired hundreds, if not thousands, of rounds using 50 grains of H-4831 and the 5-grain Unique priming charge, using it primarily as a one hundred-yard offhand target load on a cardboard ram target of the exact size used for 500-meter silhouette shooting. Recoil simulates full-throttle loads and accuracy is superb. Most important, I still have lots of that powder to burn.

If you will back up three paragraphs, note that when using the same identical load for three different weight bullets, the heaviest bullet attained the highest velocity and the next heaviest bullet, the next highest velocity. This characteristic is not unusual in the .45-70. Unlike a bottlenecked case, the straight .45-70 case does not form a restricted combustion chamber to help assure uniform and complete combustion. Instead, when using the slower burning powders in the .45-70, it is the weight of the bullet that provides the necessary resistance to obtain uniform and complete combustion. Even with the faster-burning 3031, heavier bullets often deliver higher velocity with a given load.

20

The Final Word

Even before I heard the crash of the shot or felt the little Ruger slam into my shoulder, the buck collapsed where he had stood. Slowly I got off the stump, ejected the spent case, taking care to stuff it in my pocket before shoving a fresh cartridge into the chamber. The breech snapped shut and I walked up the hill to the deer, counting the steps as I went. Forty-seven paces; a scant forty yards. Yet that abbreviated range is far more typical of North American hunting than the two hundred, three hundred and four hundred-yard shots we read about and for which most hunters equip themselves.

If I were to start all over again, knowing what I know today, I'd start right out with a good stout .45-70 rifle and never look back.

The author's Navy Arms Buffalo Rifle with tang sight and a Lyman 17A target sight on front. This is a heavy rifle weighing nearly twelve pounds, and gives fairly good accuracy with the RCBS 45-400-FN bullet and the 550-grain paper patched bullet from the Canoll mould. The internal barrel dimensions for this particular rifle are .448 inch bore and .454 inch groove — too small for flexibility with most .45-70 bullets.

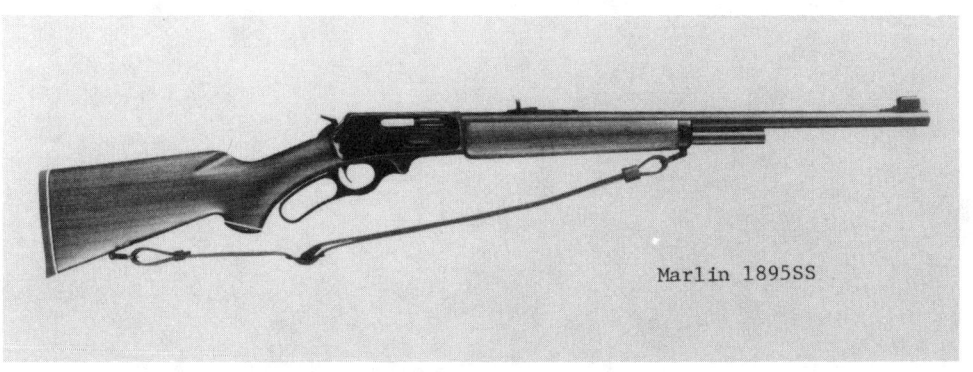

Marlin 1895SS

A recent acquisition to the author's arsenal is a Marlin 1895 .45-70. Stronger than the old Winchester 1886, the Marlin is the only .45-70 repeating rifle on the market today and is an excellent arm for brushlot deer hunting, wild boar or bear.

Although the days of prairie blackened with buffalo are long gone, the Navy Arms Buffalo Rifle and cross-sticks still carry the flavor of the old days when pig lead and black powder were king.

21

Letters

When I first started taking rifles seriously, I found myself in a school of confusion; big bore versus small bore, .270 versus .30-06, and high velocity light bullets versus the lower velocity heavier bullets of the same caliber. It seemed that there were no definitive answers, so I wrote letters and I asked questions as only a novice can ask them. Then I tried to separate the wheat from the chaff.

The letters that follow are in reply to those questions of so long ago, most of them pertaining to the .45-70. I felt the letters so important, so enlightening even though they sometimes added to the confusion, that I saved them for almost forty years. Rather than risk the loss of these nuggets of lore from men whose field of expertise far exceeded my own, I offer them here to those who never had the opportunity to correspond with such giants of the gun community.

THE

1600 RHODE ISLAND AVENUE ··· WASHINGTON 6, D.C.

ELMER KEITH
Salmon, Idaho

Jan 23rd.

Mr. Paul A. Mathhews
R.D.No 2,
Athens Penna.

Dear Mr. Mathews :

        The first word on page 13 of my article Sixguns should have read inadequate as I originally wrote it and I wrote Mr. Scofield and asked for a correction of this in the next issue as soon as I read it. The 32-20 certainly proved inadequate for mule deer for me and I so wrote it up.
        I never did claim that any sixgun was adequate for elk and grizzly, merely told what had been done with them in the hands of very expert hunters and skilled sixgun shots. You know and I know that an old Woodsman can and does kill game cleanly with no crips with both sixguns and rifles of inadequate power, but when the hunting army takes the field each fall there is not over 5% of them experienced hunters and only about that many can trail game without snow.
        Also if you kill enough elk you will see some of them absorb a gun full of light high velocity bullets and then take off in a run and if enough other elk ross the trail or if its raining or snowing hard enough at the same time you will very often lose them entirely. A paunch hit from the 06 wont stop them with any bullet. I hit one a raking shot with the 06 and 220 grain into paunch in 1917 and trailed that bull from daylight until nearly dark before I finished him. Yet I have seen many paunced with both the 300 grain 375 magnum and also the 405 "inchester and none of them went over 200 yards before stopping and were easily approached and finished, they ere simply too sick from the impact of the heavy slug to travel. I also hot some in the paunch in running shooting with the 400 Whelen and none went over 100 yards. I have now killed 33 elk muself for my own use not counting crips finished for others and seen well over 200 head killed probably nearer 300 head all told and I believe you will find my recommendations right for elk if you hunt them long enough.
        If the dudes close their eyes and flinch at the shot they are still better off with a magnum 375 as a gut shot from it will stop a buck or slow up an elk also and leave a blood trail whereit wont from a small bore. You probably will not agree with me now but after you kill as much game as I have and see as much killed you will agree with me 100 %. Better a damn sight to miss by flinching with a big caliber than to paunch them with a small one. Think that over. They shoot a 12 bore all day on ducks and think nothing of it yet expect to kill our largest game with the smallest possible rifle and it dont make sense to me. Sincerely, Keith.

PLEASE ADDRESS ALL QUESTIONS TO "DOPE BAG" NATIONAL RIFLE ASSOCIATION, 1600 RHODE ISLAND AVENUE, N. W., WASHINGTON 6, D. C.
PUBLISHED MONTHLY BY THE NATIONAL RIFLE ASSOCIATION OF AMERICA

THE American Rifleman

1600 RHODE ISLAND AVENUE ··· WASHINGTON 6, D.C.

ELMER KEITH
Salmon, Idaho

July 16th

Mr. Paul A. Matthews,
R.D. #2,
Athens, Penna.

Dear Mr. Matthews:

       That Ackley rebarrelled 45-70 model '86 should make you the best possible brush gun for deer or any game on this continent for that matter.
       I believe you can use 54 grains 3031 with the Gould bullet as 3031 is a better powder than 4064 for the straight case and get about 1900 to 2000 feet and would suggest if you use a wad you cast them a trifle softer about one to 16 tin and lead for better expansion and that Gould hollow point will then be very destructive and will surely stop any deer. I prefer the 405 grain soft point as it will destroy less meat but where there are a lot of imitation hunters in the hills who will stoop to tag anothers rightful game then it behooves one to drop them cold and am sure you will find the 45-70 outfit will do it better and quicker than any 06 but be sure if possible to get them in the ribs and stay clear of the quarters or it will destroy some meat. The 405 grain is not bad on stew but unless speeded up much faster than factory loadings will let a deer run a couple hundred yards with lung shots.
       Most of folks disagree with me and get quite peeved at my recommendations but after a bit more experience they come back and agree and find I was right and it has ever been my policy to write of actual experiences not arm chair theories, so I just put down the facts however screwy they may sound and let the chips fall where they may. You are on the right track for timber hunting. Best wishes,

                                                 Sincerely,
                                                 Keith.

P.S. 54 grains 4895 also works well with 405 grain factory soft point or cast bullets or lighter weight like the Gould.

THE American Rifleman

1600 RHODE ISLAND AVENUE ··· WASHINGTON 6, D.C.

ELMER KEITH
Salmon, Idaho

Feb 8th-52.

Mr. Paul A. Mathews,
R.D,#2,
Athens, Penna.

Dear Mr. Matthews:

           That was a very good performance on that doe for a rather low velocity load as a low heart or lung shot is never the quick kill r that a high heart or lung shot is. This for the reason the animal simply bleeds out. If a high heart shot the aorta is busted and the big blood vessels give a hydraulic shock to the whole blood system when so hit and a high lung shot also soon fills the chest cavity with blood to the extent there is no room for normal functioning of the lungs and the beast suffocates, while with the low shot it simply bleeds to death and this takes longer. Both however are certain. However I often wonder at some of the tales told by many old timers including Bell on his African elephant killing and of his killing elephant with 7 M M solids with heart shots when old Gordon Cumming put 30 to 40, balls into an elephants chest from 8 and ten bore guns before getting them down.
           Like you I like the 150 grain expanding 06 load for open country deer shooting, it is darn good but for timber I do not like it andmuch preferthe 45-70 and God knows have killed and seen killed more big game than all our present American arms commentators put together and I am still learning.
           You can eliminate that tallow wad in your load and cut the black out entirely and use 4895 by lubricating the Postell bullet. I knew that slugs as a 525 grain so you must have ordered it with one band removed. Probably you could use 45 to possibly 50 grains 4895 if you have a good nickel or hard steel barrel and that would flat en trajectory. In my experience 45-70 rifles have always shown best accuracy with 500 to 525 grain bullets andthe big Sharps with 550 to 566 grain slugs.
           Making a double rifle is a hell of an undertaking but I wish you luck. It has been done and can be done again. Oneil made one up in 44-40 I believe just to see if he could lay the two barrels toegther and did it alright. The fitting and sweating of ribs so barrel will group together is the big chore after breech fitted to action. Personally I dont care whether letters come direct or through the Rifleman but it would be better if you sent them in to Rifleman as that is the way they want it done andthey then have record of it all Likewise they also wantvto divide up letters between us so some of us dont get all the work. Best wishes,

                                        Sincerely, Keith

NATIONAL RIFLE ASSOCIATION OF AMERICA
Publishers of **THE AMERICAN RIFLEMAN**

1600 Rhode Island Avenue, N. W. • Washington 6, D. C. DIstrict 3412

May 1, 1952

Mr. Paul A. Matthews
R. D. #2,
Athens, Pennsylvania

Dear Mr. Matthews:

Your idea of building a double rifle chambered for the .45/70 cartridge is entirely practical but I am afraid that the cost of such a weapon would be very high. For my money, your best bet would be to use the Model 21 Winchester double as a basis for this arm. Whether or not Winchester would make up a set of .45/70 barrels and fit them to the 21 action is another story, however. I believe that an expert gunsmith could reline the barrels of a Model 21 with tubes rifled and chambered for the .45/70 cartridge but, here again, you are running into an expensive project. The only thing I can suggest, then, is that you write to Winchester to see if they would be interested in tackling the problem.

There is also the slim possibility that you may be able to obtain a set of Belgian made barrels for fitting to a Model 21 Winchester, but I must admit this is only a shot in the dark on my part. Why don't you write to Mr. Rodney Day, Exeter Road, Haverford, Pennsylvania to see if he can offer you any assistance in this matter. Mr. Day is importing fine Belgian made barrels for fitting to the older Damascus steel shotguns and it is just possible that he may be able to arrange for a set of .45/70 rifle barrels at a reasonable price.

There is no doubt in my mind that one of the larger English gun firms such as Westley Richards could build you a double rifle chambered for the .45/70 cartridge, but I am afraid that the price would be in the vicinity of $1000.00, since their weapons are literally handmade from buttplate to muzzle.

Let me know how you come out in your search and I may be able to give you some more leads in the event you run up against the proverbial brick wall.

Sincerely yours,

NATIONAL RIFLE ASSOCIATION

M. D. Waite
NRA Technical Service

MDW/mb

THE American Rifleman

1600 RHODE ISLAND AVENUE ··· WASHINGTON 6, D. C.

ELMER KEITH
Salmon, Idaho

Aug 25th.

Mr. Paul A. Matthews,
R D # 2,
Athens, Penna:

Dear Mr. Matthews:

   Believe if you can get this cork gasket material and cut wads from it they will be even better than the greased felt wad under your 330 gould bullet because a cartridge loaded for any length of time may absorb some of that grese in the powder and thus ruin your load. I like greased felt hat wads cap and ball sixguns with black powder but use tallow or beeswax tht wont melt but believe if the bullet is well lubricated that a cork wad is better to help protect base of bullet from the gas and imprint of the powder grains.
   The old case hardened '86 actions are good for 38,000 pounds pressure and the newer heat treated blued receivers and I have one under 125,000 are good for 42,000 they claim or about same as the model 71 claims but I personally think the 71 action stronger than any '86.
   You have no fear about pressures in that load of 54 grains 3031 and the 330 Gould bullet as it does not go over 30,000 pounds. However a bum case can crop up and I have had one instance broughtvto my notice of a Rem case cracking half way around just in front of the rim and I have that case here now. It let out enough gas to blow the loading gate out and caususe some action damage but none to the shooter, purely a bum case and all 45-70 cases I have seen are the protruding primer pocket type and not as strong in the head as they should be but we have fired many hundreds of them with no trouble. Stongest thickest 45-70 cases I have seen were F.A. nickeled cases made in '91
   Also heard of one more blow up and have the cases that proves it had excessive headspace and was not properly re-barrelled. as cuts for the cartridge fingers were made square and left no supporting chamber walls over that portion of the case. In neither case did the breech bolt dome unlocked and both merely let gas into bottom action and blew out loading gate, My load of 54 grains 3031 and the 405 grain soft point is a heavier pressure load than what you are using and we use in in an old case hardened action and two of the later blued actions.
   Shipped you autographee copy of my rifle book yesterday. Best wishes,

                Sincerely
                Keith.

THE American Rifleman

1600 RHODE ISLAND AVENUE ··· WASHINGTON 6, D.C.

ELMER KEITH
Salmon, Idaho

Sept 8th-52

Mr. Paul A. Mathhews,
R.D. No 2,
Athens, Penna.

Dear Mr. Matthews:

        You will have a very hard time ever finding a better brush gun for deer and elk than the 45-70 featherweight model '86 Winchester or a better killing deer load in the brush than 54 grains 3031 and the 330 Gould hollow point cast bullet. For elk the 405 grain soft point or solid cast is better. with same powder load. If all timber deer hunters used them instead 270s and 06s we would have a lot more deer left alive for the next hunting season and the hunter kill would be much larger also that is the ones the actually get.
        You and I are about same heighth but I am heavier my own dimensions on my stock design are drop at point of Monte Carlo cheek piece comb 1 5/8" and at ~~heelxtxtxxxxxxx~~ bump or rear end Monte 1½" and at heel 2¼" and length from trigger to center butt plate 13 3/8", Trigger to grip cap 3" and down pitch of one to two inches.
        E.C.B shop, Warsaw, Mo makes my stock design, either as regular stock or in the Custom Dept under Nathan Bishop. I do not know if Hutchins has this design or not. Also Iver Henrikson 1220 So. 2nd St, Missoula, Mont. used my design for his fine French walnut custom stocks.
        Harold Johnson, Coopers landing, Alaska also uses my stock design and makes a heavy 450 calibre rifle from the 348 with 348 case and gets around 2000 ft or more with 405 grain bullet from the 348 case straightened out to 450 and claims its one of finest bear rifles he has yet found for the brush and alders.
        A Williams Fool Proof receiver sight and a Sourdough front is one swell combination for the timber on that proposed 375. A.J.Ashurst, Salmon, Idaho can make you a good bbl in that caliber to your order also stock it as well if you wish.
        The 375 is the best commercial all around ctg for all big game hunting I know of today. Its superbly accurate with full or reduced loads and one man in Penn whom I recommended it to years ago wrote me over a year ago he had now killed around 40 head of game and all with one shot each which is a far cry from the results of the 270 boys.
        Bob Wallack, Mayfield, N.Y. I believe or C/o The American Rifleman can furnish you a good rifle on your action or so can Harold McFarland, Prescott, Ariz.

                                        Sincerely,
                                        Keith

PLEASE ADDRESS ALL QUESTIONS TO "DOPE BAG" NATIONAL RIFLE ASSOCIATION, 1600 RHODE ISLAND AVENUE, N. W., WASHINGTON 6, D. C.
PUBLISHED MONTHLY BY THE NATIONAL RIFLE ASSOCIATION OF AMERICA

THE American Rifleman

1600 RHODE ISLAND AVENUE ··· WASHINGTON 6, D.C.

ELMER KEITH
Salmon, Idaho

Jan 16th-53.

Mr. Paul A, Matthews,
R.D.#2,
Athens, ~~Stxtx~~ Penna.

Dear Mr. Matthews:

You have a darn good 375 though is much heavier than I would want to carry. I once put 16 consecutive shots Winchester 300 grain soft point factory 375 magnum into just one and nine sixteenths inches at 200 yards prone with sling and no rest and 330 "eaver post reticule scope in Stith mounts 24" bbl straight taper model 70 rifle they gaveme. center to center of widest holes.
The 375 mag will lick most smaller calibers at 200 yards i if you can hold it.including many bull gun 06s
You cant beat that old 45-70 '86 ,model for a timber gun for anything on this contineet with my heavy loads. Its light fast nd handy and kills and also leaves a blood trail which a 270 almost never does.
For 375 mag loads try Ideal gas check No 375449 - 278 gr. with 47 grains 4895 or 3031 (forty-seven grains) for a deer load and for 100 yard group shooting.
For heavy game elk, moose and grizzly try the 350 grain abrnes with 75 grains 4350 andyou then have a load for them. (seventy-five grains) also a 70 grain (seventy) is very good with same bullet and not quite so fast. Barnes uses 78 (seventy-eight grains) which I think on the heavy side. Glad you like the big rifle and some frifnds have been wining many truhey matches with them .

Sincerely
Keith.

THE

1600 RHODE ISLAND AVENUE ··· WASHINGTON 6, D.C.

ELMER KEITH
Salmon, Idaho

Jan 24th-53.

Mr. Paul A. Matthews,
R.D.#2,
Athens, Ohio.

Dear Mr. Matthews,

    I do not know why your letter was sent to me for answering but want to thank you for a darn good letter anyway. Like myself you learned the hard way and I still remember back in 1917 when I was a lad and followed all the Gun writings of Whelen Crossman, Curtiss et al and swallowed and believed all they wrote until the damn 30-06 let me down miserably on elk several times and then I went back to my old Sharps Creedmoor and business picked up at once. I was hunting for meat to eat and regularly kept our family in meat as well as some widows with large families as well and when I did get a shot I wanted results at both ends of the damn gun and the old Sharps produced same for me.
    I think Mr. Musicks article oneof the best that was ran last year in front section of the Rifleman, but many small bores addicts who have had very little experience will pan him but you can tell if they do they lack experience as no experienced man is going to pan another hunter for using a big gun.
    We have just five of those 45-70 model 86 light weight rifles at this house so you can see what we think of them, only a fine double hammerless ejector rifle in suitable caliber has anything on them for timber shooting. However we dont take them to the Pahsimeroi for antelope or eagles and coyotes but for timber hunting only.
    If all hunters would learn as you have, then we would have a much larger game supply the next year as they would not wound and waste three or four for every one they bag each year.
Sincerely and with all best wishes,

                                        Keith.

PLEASE ADDRESS ALL QUESTIONS TO "DOPE BAG" NATIONAL RIFLE ASSOCIATION, 1600 RHODE ISLAND AVENUE, N. W., WASHINGTON 6, D. C.
PUBLISHED MONTHLY BY THE NATIONAL RIFLE ASSOCIATION OF AMERICA

P.O. Ackley Incorporated
Trinidad, Colorado

Federal License No.

August 24, 1951

MAKERS OF
Ackley Barrels
Ackley Snap-On Mounts
Ackley Magnum Rifles
Precision Scope Mounting
Practical Conversions
Barrel Blanks
Special Parts
Expert Repairing
Ackley Low-Line Safety
Controlled Expansion Bullets

Paul A. Matthews
RD #2
Athens, Penna.

Dear Sir:

We have never re-heatreated any Winchester 86 actions. However all of the old actions drill like a piece of cheese. I have never seen one with any real case on it. You can use any normal loads in the rifle which is recommended for the .45-70 cartridge. The Model 86 cannot be overloaded very much without the cartridges sticking. That is, if you over load the cases a little bit the action will stay locked. This will occur a long time before dangerous loads are reached.

I am sure that you will find your Mod. 86 perfectly normal in every respect. When these actions are blued, of course the outside case hardening glaze is removed. This in no way affects the heat treatment.

Very truly yours,

P.O. Ackley, Inc.

poa;jr
voice written

WINCHESTER REPEATING ARMS COMPANY
DIVISION OF OLIN INDUSTRIES, INC.
NEW HAVEN, 4, CONNECTICUT, U.S.A.
WINCHESTER
TRADE MARK

August 14, 1951

Mr. Paul A. Matthews
R. D. 2
Athens, Pennsylvania

Dear Mr. Matthews:

No doubt by the time this letter arrives you will have received our telegram in which we warned you against the hand loads for your Model 86, 45-70 caliber rifle, serial number 73178.

In further explanation, the Model 86 rifles with serial numbers below 126,000 were all fitted with case hardened receivers (or frames) which were sufficiently rugged for the black powder loads and later the semi-smokeless loads in use up to 1903.

At that time, the 33 W.C.F. cartridge was developed using smokeless powder and the Model 1886 rifle was adapted to this cartridge by changing the frame to blued steel.

Only Model 86 rifles, therefore, with serial numbers above 126,000 would be considered safe with high velocity loads such as you mention.

Our present 45-70, 405 cartridge is loaded with low pressure powder only and we definitely do not recommend the use of any cartridges loaded to higher velocities than standard factory loads.

We hope you will accept our warning in the very friendly spirit in which it is offered. Our first and foremost consideration has always been the personal safety of our many sportsmen friends.

                              Very truly yours,

                              WINCHESTER REPEATING ARMS COMPANY
                              Division of Olin Industries, Inc.

                              F. P. James
                              Sales Department

FPJ:dpl

2660A

THE American Rifleman

1600 RHODE ISLAND AVENUE ··· WASHINGTON 6, D. C.

PHILIP B. SHARPE
Staff Writer

23 Jan 52

Mr, Paul A Mathews
Route 2
Athens, Pa.

Dear Mr. Mathews:

When I told you to write me a "few weeks after Christmas" I did not anticipate the weather. I live in Pennsylvania, too, and I think you will agree with me that this is not shooting weather.

I have not been inspired to shoot those smokeless 45/70 loads. Would you tramp through snow and mud on a range in this weather, changing targets, and chronographing the stuff--anything? Last year at this time I was shooting.

I note that you want to use these UMC cases for reloading with heavy loads in your Model 86. Better think again. You fire them and throw them away or you pull bullets and decap the cases. They are primed with a mercuric primer and were loaded for the Government for use in a Gattling gun. They should be safe in your 86, but not after reloading *as these primers are used*

So you want to get your 1300 f.s. rifle into 1900 f.s.? Please, may I beg out? I have no recommendations in making a Magnum out of a gun designed over 65 years ago.

Cordially,

Phil Sharpe

EX-1221

E. I. du Pont de Nemours & Company
INCORPORATED
PENNS GROVE, N. J.

EXPLOSIVES DEPARTMENT
BURNSIDE LABORATORY

ADDRESS ALL CORRESPONDENCE TO
BURNSIDE LABORATORY
POST OFFICE BOX 152
PENNS GROVE, N. J.

May 28, 1952

Mr. Paul A. Matthews
R. D. 2
Athens, Pennsylvania

Dear Sir:

      Your letter of May 21, 1952 has been referred to this Laboratory for reply.

      We are listing our various powders that are packed in canisters in accordance with their burning rates, the first being the fastest:

Rank	Powder Number
1	I.M.R. 4227
2	" 4198
3	" 3031
4	" 4064
5	" 4320
6	" 4350

      We do not have comparative burning rates of Hercules powders and, therefore, cannot give you any information on how Sharpshooter compares with our powders. We believe that it is their fastest burning powder, but have no idea how it compares with our I.M.R. 4227.

      In view of the fact that you report a flatter trajectory with the 300-grain bullet in the 45/70 with 30.0 grains of I.M.R. 4227 than you formerly obtained with the factory-loaded cartridge, it is our opinion that you should not exceed this weight of charge as you are probably getting pressures near the high limit. It might be well to reduce the charge to the point where the trajectory equals that of the factory load for the sake of safety.

Very truly yours,

BURNSIDE LABORATORY

W. H. Coxe

WHC:ml
5

150TH ANNIVERSARY
BETTER THINGS FOR BETTER LIVING ... THROUGH CHEMISTRY

EX-1221

E. I. du Pont de Nemours & Company
INCORPORATED
PENNS GROVE, N. J.

EXPLOSIVES DEPARTMENT
BURNSIDE LABORATORY

ADDRESS ALL CORRESPONDENCE TO
BURNSIDE LABORATORY
POST OFFICE BOX 152
PENNS GROVE, N. J.

June 6, 1952

Mr. Paul A. Matthews
RD# 2
Athens, Pa.

Dear Sir:

       In answer to your letter of June 21, 1952, sharpshooter powder is a double-base powder made of nitrocellulose and nitroglycerine while du Pont I.M.R. 4227 is made of nitrocellulose and is termed a single-base powder. Double-base powders burn at a higher temperature than single-base powders and hence develop more erosion of the barrels and tend to lead the barrels more. This explains the differences you noted in your tests of the two powders.

       Thank you for sending the results of your "handloaders comparison" to us.

Very truly yours,

BURNSIDE LABORATORY

W. H. Coxe

WHC:GMB

150TH ANNIVERSARY
BETTER THINGS FOR BETTER LIVING ... THROUGH CHEMISTRY

Outdoor Life
First Choice of Discriminating Sportsmen

353 FOURTH AVENUE · NEW YORK 10, N.Y.

ARMS & AMMUNITION DEPT.
JACK O'CONNOR, EDITOR

Paul A. Matthews
R. D. #2
Athens, Penna.

Dec. 18, 1951

Dear Mr. Matthews:

Yes, I agree with you that the old Indian guide who said "Any gun good, shoot 'em good" had something on the ball.

If you placed properly that 150-gr. bullet from the .30/06 I do not see how you could fail to kill a deer quickly. By that I mean most of the time but some very strange things happen. How much game I have killed with the 150-gr. load in the .30/06, I'll be darned if I know but I do know that I have killed with it a good many mule and whitetail deer, a fair number of sheep and antelope. At least three-fourths of the deer and antelope I have shot with that have been either dead in their tracks or within a jump or two.

Step the 300-gr. bullet in the .45/70 up to 1800--2000 f.p.s. and you have really got quite a cannon but that is a far cry from the standard factory load at 1300 f.p.s.

My best wishes,

JACK O'CONNOR

kif

Conservation Pledge
I GIVE MY PLEDGE AS AN AMERICAN TO SAVE AND FAITHFULLY
TO DEFEND FROM WASTE THE NATURAL RESOURCES OF MY COUNTRY —
ITS SOIL AND MINERALS, ITS FORESTS, WATERS AND WILDLIFE

IN OUR SCHOOLS — IN ALL ASSEMBLIES OF AMERICANS — LET THIS PLEDGE RING OUT!

NATIONAL RIFLE ASSOCIATION OF AMERICA
Publishers of THE AMERICAN RIFLEMAN
1600 Rhode Island Avenue · Washington 6, D. C.   District 3412

Technical Division

September 27, 1949

Mr. Paul A. Matthews
Route 2
Athens, Pennsylvania

Dear Mr. Matthews:

    I would certainly start with a charge several grains under the maximum recommended if I wanted good accuracy in my .30-'06 rifle. I would also try different bullets such as the Hornady and Sierra 180 grain, as you do not know which will work best in your rifle. I cannot understand why you have selected No. 3031 for the heavy bullets in .30-'06 caliber, as No. 4064 works very well and so does No. 4350, as we indicated in our pressure data in the April issue of THE AMERICAN RIFLEMAN.

    Unless you want to seat bullets out to touch the rifling you should seat them for an overall length of 3.34 inches so that they will work through the magazine. For strict accuracy we seat bullets farther out and then handload them singly. When you use a greater seating depth you will naturally have to stay away from the extreme maximum loads, but after all the maximum powder charge which you can use does not always give you the best accuracy. I would say that 49 to 50 grains Dupont No. 4064 or 54 to 56 grains No. 4350 might make the best combination for your 180-grain bullets.

                                                    Cordially,

                                                  A. H. Barr,
B/MR   Technical Division.

NATIONAL RIFLE ASSOCIATION OF AMERICA
Publishers of THE AMERICAN RIFLEMAN
1600 Rhode Island Avenue · Washington 6, D. C.   DIstrict 3412

Technical Division

December 23, 1949

Mr. Paul A. Matthews
R. D. #2, Athens, Pa.

Dear Mr. Matthews:

      I can tell you with all sincerity that I enjoyed your letter very much, and this despite the fact that most of us are inclined to shudder when we see a really long letter coming to the top of the pile while answering Dope Bag correspondence. As you probably know, we often answer as many as 100 letters a day in an effort to keep our heads above water. By the end of the day (which can run as long as 16 hours) we become a bit frazzled and frayed at the edges. In spite of all this, I can tell you that you do have a knack for writing in an interesting manner, and I can honestly say that I enjoyed every sentence and paragraph of your letter. I would certainly recommend that you think about writing some articles for THE RIFLEMAN, if you ever have the time and opportunity. As a constant reader of our magazine, you are more or less familiar with the type of manuscript which pleases our Editor, and I would therefore recommend that you dream up a good subject and do something about it.

      As a man interested in guns, you would enjoy looking over some of the correspondence received at this office, which would indicate that many of our sportsmen though very much interested in such subjects as handloading have absolutely no idea of the problems involved. Many of these people are absolutely helpless when confronted with a powder measure and loading press despite the fact that they have been burning powder since they have kicked the slats out of a cradle. The fact that you have been able to solve your own reloading difficulties speaks well for your ingenuity and common sense, but I am afraid that many of our members are not so gifted. We are continually shaking in our shoes when we read some of the dope that comes into this office via correspondence. In other words, some of our members take case capacity literally and as far as they are concerned, all gun powders are alike in potential. As I dictated that last sentence, I glanced at the floor where one well-smashed up Ross rifle is now reclining. I don't know for sure what happened, but if it wasn't an overload, I don't know what it was! The gentleman in question is suffering no pain at the present time.

Mr. Paul A. Matthews	-2-	December 23, 1949

    The front sight described in your letter is quite similar to the Dockendorff which is now commercially available and which utilizes very fine gold-plated cross wires or cross wires in conjunction with a small bead. The cross wire in the Dockendorff sight is slanted back at an angle of 15 degrees in order to improve contrast under various light conditions. This sight is also fitted with a sliding sleeve in order to vary the amount of light entering into the tube itself. I personally have never taken one of these Dockendorff sights into the hunting field, but the principle is certainly sound, and I can see why you have become well satisfied with your design.

    Thanks again for your interesting letter and if you ever get down to Washington, don't hesitate to call on us here for a little visit.

                      Cordially yours,

                      NATIONAL RIFLE ASSOCIATION

                      M. D. Waite
                      NRA Technical Service

MDW/elf

32 BLACKTHORN LANE
WHITE PLAINS, N. Y.

Jan. 10, 1953.

Dear Paul,

Thank you for yours of Dec. 31. Harry had mentioned some of your g.c. load data. Those are loads which I work out for unusual calibers only, now. They are pretty much in the nature of insurance only, as the jacketed bullets are available. But, back in the '30s, when time was more plentifull and money the reverse, the cast and g.c. loads were used for most of my shooting, except for big game. I had fewer rifles but enjoyed myself quite as much, and if it were not for the experimental work, Bert Shay, Phil Sharpe and I are constantly getting into, I'd as soon do as I did in the '30s. On the loads I work out in each caliber, as soon as I get 2" groups at 100, I'm satisfied as in a pinch, they'll do for close work on game — they have (these loads run 1600-1700 f.s. in most instances, when chronographed), killed deer on trials in several calibers. These loads are made with 85% lead, 10% tin and 5% antimony, as that alloy has been satisfactory for them.

If I had the time, I'd look into the results of a lead-tin-zinc alloy for highspeed (over 1700 f.s.) g.c. loads. In the old literature on hunting dangerous game in India and Africa, quite a few hunters, whose names are legendary to-day, mention the hardening of their cast bullets with zinc for their heavy charges of black, in rifles which later, became known as "expresses". The charges they used (Sir Samuel Baker for example), certainly gave closer to 2000 f.s. than 1600 f.s. and the zinc may have been the detail in those loads, that made the high velocity attainable. It is worth looking into. Your 8-1-1 alloy may do as well but I doubt it as Naramore states that more than 5% of antimony in a cast-bullet alloy, tends to make a bullet brittle, so shearing by the lands is likely.

We do know that our 85-10-5 alloy will handle 1700 f.s. or so, but give it any more speed and the leading at the muzzle shows and the group starts to spread out.

In the .308 Win. tests, reported by Phil in the Jan. Rifleman, there were some tests made, which proved nothing in particular and were not pertinent to the .308, so the data was not published. I've extracted it from my notes as they may mean something to you. All Bert, Phil and I know, is that is what the chronograph said. So, you can see there's plenty of work still to be done on g.c. loads. Good luck to you.

Sincerely,
Tom Flanich.

Same gas check loads (two) used in .308 .30-30 and .30-06 (in one instance and in the .308 and .30-06 in another). Oct. 1952. All instrumentals are at 60 feet. Federal 210 primers used with 85-10-5 alloy bullets.

Load #1 — 160 grain G.C., 20.6 grains of 4198. This load does nicely in most any .30 cal. case, or grouping

20" barrel .30-30   1669 M.I.V.   1 turn in 12"
26"   "   "   1671   "   "   "   "

Note that 6" of barrel, shows no velocity increase so we judge the 4198 burns completely in the 20" bbl.

22½" barrel .308 Win   1596 M.I.V.   1 in 10" (Mauser)
22"   "   .308 "   1530   "   1 in 12" (M70)
21½"   "   .308 "   1611   "   1 in 14" (Mauser)

Here the twist, which varies 40% appears to have no effect on velocity

24" barrel .30-06   1524 M.I.V.   1 in 10" (Springfield)

Load #2 — 195 gr. g.c   30.4 grains of 4895 (L27277)
This is about all the 4895 you can use in the '06, with this bullet and stay in 2" @ 100 yds.

24" barrel 30-06   1663 M.I.V.   1 in 10" (Springfield)

22½" " .308 Win   1831   "   1 in 10" (Mauser)
22"   "   "   1845   "   1 in 12" (M70)
22½" "   "   1859   "   1 in 14" (Mauser)

In the .308 Win. this load does not group in 2" as it does in the '06